71.042
18s

# Surviving Home-Schooling Through the Corona Crisis

# Surviving Home-Schooling Through the Corona Crisis

Wendy Hamilton

ZealAus Publishing

Surviving Home-Schooling Through the Corona Crisis

.

ISBN: 978-1-925888-84-3 (e)

ISBN: 978-1-925888-85-0 (hc)

ISBN: 978-1-925888-86-7 (sc)

# Dedicated

To all the mothers who have embarked

on the unexpected journey of home-schooling.

May you gain from it an unexpected reward.

# Contents

# Introduction

Coronavirus has tipped the world upside down.

"Well, today was my last day at work," says my daughter, throwing her car keys on the bench. "I'm officially on stand down."

Her sister is seated at the dining room table painting the cover of her latest book, 'The Great Toilet Paper Famine.'

"Oh well, you can finish writing your book," she says, painting a wheelbarrow red. "It will be like the old days when we were homes-schooled. Mark's got one more day at Uni before all his courses go online, and Joe's been told to work from home."

"New Zealand is in complete lockdown," interrupts my husband, looking up from his phone. "If we want to go back, we will be quarantined in a hotel room for a month."

"Oh, my goodness, that would be a prison," I say. "If our parents die, we won't be able to go to the funeral."

"Yeah, we'd get there be three weeks too late."

Hannah pulls her phone out of her pocket, makes a few strategic taps and moves her thumb over the screen. She stops as something catches her attention. "One man is quarantined with a four-year-old."

"A whole month in a tiny room with a squirrelly kid," I burst out, "I hope they at least have a balcony."

I try to imagine ways to keep a young child occupied in a bare room for twenty-eight days and fail.

Hannah scrolls down a bit. "The New South Wales schools are closing until the end of the term, and Victoria has announced schools will be shut the following term as well."

Marie puts the last dab of red on the wheelbarrow. "I heard Kate and William have taken their children out of school and Kate is going to home-school," she says, starting on a whimsical mouse.

"Britain will follow their lead," I say. "I never thought I would see the day home-schooling was widespread. When I started twenty-five years ago it was looked down on.

"Listen to this," says Mark, "one expert is telling parents to dress their children in their school uniforms and stick to the normal routine!"

I am horrified. "Are you serious?"

"Yup. And they are going to put school online."

I shudder. "Oh, those poor mothers, they will be exhausted after two days. This is an area where the experts don't have a clue. The guy who said that has obviously not done a day of home-schooling in his life. What works in school will not work at home."

"How many days did you home-school, Mum?"

I look at the ceiling as I try to tot it up. "Three-hundred and sixty-five times ten equals three thousand-six-hundred-and-fifty."

"That's only ten years, you have to double it."

I'm not good at mental sums, so I guess. "A bit over seven thousand days."

"You counted the weekends," says Mark.

"When you home-school there is not much difference," I say with vim.

"Some of my friends on social media are counting up the hours the kids are at school, and deducting time for recess," says Hannah, "they think they have to teach them for five hours a day."

"Five hours! That is ridiculous, they will never manage."

Now I am really distressed for the mothers of the world. Everyone is focusing on the children, and school resources on the internet are growing like toadstools in a damp log. Forty-thousand lesson plans are all very well if you don't have resistant kids, a house to run, a toddler, and a teething baby.

Two houses away, a woman's voice lifts in frustrated anger. Her words are caught by the wind and blow over our fence.

"YOU KIDS CAN STOP YOUR FIGHTING AND GET OUTSIDE!"

People with lifeboats have a duty to save the drowning.

"I have got to help these poor women," I say, flicking open my laptop, "I have to tell them there is an easy way to home-school."

# I Didn't Want to Home-School Either

**Welcome to the world of home-schooling. A world you never expected to enter but one the corona crisis has forced on you. Right now, your children probably feel the schools closing is evidence God answers prayers. You, however, are not sharing their enthusiasm. You didn't want to home-school and never in your wildest dreams thought you would have to. Your home is suddenly a school for an indefinite length of time and you don't know what to do.**

Back in 1995, I felt like you. I didn't want to home-school. I came in contact with the idea through a neighbour whose eldest daughter was the same age as mine. I thought it was a terrible idea. I thought her kids would end up uneducated and couldn't wait until my talkative child was out of the house for six glorious hours. While she started looking at teaching programs, I enrolled my four-year-old daughter, Marie, in preschool. It was only two hours an afternoon, not the six-hour break I was looking forward to in the future, but it was a step in the right direction, or so I thought.

**Preschool was not the oasis I expected.** I felt chained. I could not go to my sister's place or the beach for the day, because every afternoon I had to take Marie to Kindergarten. Also, getting there on time was stressful. Moreover, it interfered with my two-year-old's afternoon sleep. I hated putting Hannah down later than usual and waking her early because I had to pick up Marie. Nevertheless, I rushed through lunch, cleaned up the kids, got out the stroller, found the baby bag, made sure my 'voluntary' donation was in my purse, locked the house, and half-ran two blocks to the Kindergarten. By the time I got there my face was red and my blood pressure up. Things did not improve when I was given books of raffle tickets to sell and expected to bake a cake.

The pressure to help fundraise was another thing I hadn't anticipated. Neither was the nasty feeling of losing touch with my daughter.

"What did you do today?"

"Stuff."

That was strange. My chatterbox usually talked so much it drove me nutty. I tried again.

"Did you play with the dolls?"

"A bit."

"Did you paint?"

She looked bored and shrugged.

"Did you play in the sandpit?

"I suppose."

I looked at her in concern. A mere two words, not the normal two-hundred words.

A butterfly flitted past and she brightened."Look at the butterfly Mummy, why is he so orange? If I painted myself orange, could I fly?"

She jabbered all the way home about the butterfly.

One day after I dropped Marie off, I stopped just outside the fence and watched her. I saw that instead of finger-painting or playing in the sandpit calmly, she flitted erratically around the many activities available in a frenzied rush of overstimulation. When I got home, I put Hannah (who was grizzling with over-tiredness) into bed.

## Surviving Home-Schooling Through the Corona Crisis

Usually, I had an afternoon sleep myself to recharge my batteries for the evening pit hour of dinner, baths, and bed but I was afraid of oversleeping so instead, I made a cup of tea and flicked through a magazine.

About that time, a small wave of home-schooling was washing through the churches and some of my friends were getting on board. I was still not keen, but by now I realized there was a cost to handing my child over to others. The turning point was the day she stole a picture from a small girl who shouted: "I hate you." Later that day I had a conversation with my sister during which I rattled off all the reasons I did not want to home-school, lingering at length over the horror of becoming a teacher and turning my lovely home into an ugly school.

I did, however, have to admit there were things in home-schooling's favour.

You do not lose control.

You retain your right to mould your child's character.

The days are flexible

Children are fifteen times less likely to get sick.

You don't have to tiptoe around political agendas.

You can take breaks and school holidays when it suits you.

You can work around your children's individual needs.

Children can work at the pace best for them.

You can do it anywhere, so kids don't have the trauma of starting a new school if you shift location.

You don't have the morning rush to get them off to school

Not a bad list for starters. At the end of my conversation I had decided to home-school. When I suggested the idea to my husband, he was very pleased. In fact, he admitted he was relieved, which came as a surprise to us both. As I started to seriously look into home-schooling, I discovered my belief home-schooled kids ended up uneducated was wrong. There is ample evidence home educated children outperform school children academically and socially. And if you have a world view and values you wish to pass on to the next generation, home-schooling is the best way to do it.

So armed with this knowledge, I removed my daughter from preschool and applied for a school exemption just before she turned six.

> **Despite everyone sending their children to school at five, in New Zealand, you don't have to legally send children to school until they are six.**

Back then, home-schooling was a revolutionary idea. It was common for home-schoolers to get disapproval from family members and the public because home-schooling was different. It takes courage to do something different.

**Like everyone else I tried to teach like a school at first, which was disastrous.** Many days nothing got done, and at nights just before I dropped off to sleep, I struggled with fear and guilt over my inadequacy.

---

I write about my home-schooling journey in my book 'Eating a Light Bulb Does Not Make You Bright, (Light on Home-schooling)'

---

**Thankfully, I found an easier way to teach.** Now my children are grown, I laugh about those nightly fears. I never did get the daily break I was so looking forward to because none of my children went to school. I home-schooled the four of them from Kindergarten through to university. I never turned my home into an ugly classroom and I wasn't much of a teacher, yet my kids are well-educated, intelligent adults, and I am proud of their life decisions.

Marie, the child who drove me crazy with her talking, is now an author and illustrator. Her children's books are a whimsical, quirky world of Victorian mice who live in hollow trees and have adventures.

Hannah, my-slow-to-warm-up shy child, sailed through pirate waters on a Mercy ship when she was nineteen, to work in an orphanage and clean wells in Sri Lanka. Later she looked after babies in the Wiatoto Baby Home in Uganda and now works at an airline.

Joe, the boy who spent his days pulling electronic gadgets to pieces and making booby traps to electrify his sisters, graduated from Western Sydney University in 2019 with First Class Honours in Electrical Engineering.

Mark, who spent most of his childhood playing with Lego, and was so dyslexic I gave up trying to teach him to spell, can string long lengths of computer code together. Today he attends Western Sydney University and is in his last year of a Computer Science degree.

Best of all, we are a close family, and with God's help, my husband and I have managed to pass on our values. Of all the things I have done, homes-schooling my children is the thing I am most proud of. I am glad I did it.

**The one thing I would do differently if I had my time over again, is I would worry less.**

I write this book to pass on some of the things I learnt during my twenty-year journey as a home-schooling Mum. In a home-school, it is the mother who learns the most. I learnt how children really learn, time and energy management, and setting priorities. Even more importantly, I have had to develop courage and leadership. It hasn't been easy, but it has been worth it. I hope by writing this book I will spare you from burning out, a costly and unnecessary peril.

# Summary

Like you, I did not want to home-school. It was not coronavirus that forced me into it, was a concern for my child. Too many activities were simultaneously boring and overstimulating her.

When I researched home-schooling, I discovered there are many advantages to home-schooling.

I tried many times to home-school like 'real' schools, but it was disastrous. Eventually, I found an easier way that made it possible for me to stick at home-schooling.

I home-schooled my children for over twenty years and I'm glad I did because I am pleased with the result. I learnt a lot about children and developed strength and leadership through home-schooling.

I write this book to save you from the peril of burnout.

# Emotional Roller Coasters

Deal with Your Emotions Before You Get Started

**Before we get into the practical application of home-schooling, we need to deal with your emotions.**

The rule when the Oxygen gets low in a plane is put your mask on first before you help your child. The schools are closing and everyone is focusing on the children's education.

Few people are thinking about the emotional wellbeing of the mothers, so you must take steps to take care of yourself because you are the lynchpin of the home.

If you go down and can't cope the whole family goes down. So, let's start working through the common list of negative emotions you need to conquer.

# Fear

**First, take a deep breath. Your children are safe, they are in your home and under your care.** They are healthy and not likely to get coronavirus because they won't come in contact with it. Although the world is in crisis and everything is gloom and doom, try to keep it in perspective. The world has regular crises and it keeps ongoing. Check your history. Roughly every ten years something big happens.

**Now is a good time to brush up your prayer life and trust in God.**

Second, it is frightening when your world tips upside down and you lose control of your life; especially when it is for an indefinite length of time. We all want to go back to normal, but nobody knows when that will be.

**Even though home-schooling has been thrust upon you, grasp the nettle and choose it. It will make you feel more in control.**

Making an active decision to home-school will give you the motivation to make the changes you need for the smooth running of your home. Who knows, you may even find this is a blessing in disguise.

# Socialization

This has always been the big criticism of home-schooling. **Many experts have admitted home-schooling delivers education well.** But the myth children need lots of other children to be socialized properly, remains. No doubt you are worried about this issue, especially if your child has been used to an active social life. Here comes the best part.

**Your children will become good friends with their siblings when they are the only choice they have.**

And siblings are excellent sandpaper for self-absorbed, selfish and conceited behaviour. If you home-school for any length of time, it is likely your children will start getting on better and your family will grow closer. You may even find general behaviour improves the longer your children are out of school as you have so much more control over negative peer pressure.

**Don't allow peer pressure to mould your children. If your children are spending all their time on their phones, confiscate them and let them have them at the end of the day.**

As time goes on, you may even unearth some problems like bullying in school. And troubles like bedwetting and anxiety may drop off. If home-schooling goes on for any length of time, school holidays will change from something you dread to something you look forward to, simply because the pressure to do schoolwork will be off.

# Exhaustion.

**Exhaustion is a big challenge especially for the mother of primary aged children and younger.**

**The nature of children is they are emotionally draining.** It is meant to be this way, nevertheless, it is debilitating. It is grossly unfair kids have far more energy than their mothers. I have discovered the ability to make decisions is a finite quality. If you let a talkative five-year-old bombard you with questions early in the morning, it is unlikely you will be functioning past 9 am. Despite the sentimental idea, there is no such thing as a stupid question, children are overflowing with foolish questions.

> **Nip the endless Why-game in the bud, it requires very little effort on their part to keep asking "why" and is tremendously draining for you.**

**Boost Up Your Sleep with an Afternoon Nap.**

It is an indisputable law of nature you will not have enough energy for all the tasks and responsibilities of this stage of life.

> **Many of the educational experts are offering advice as practical as throwing a lead ball into the sea and expecting it to float.**

Have the confidence to ditch anything that is not working for you (including online lessons.)

Spend your energy like a miser who counts the cost of every transaction.

Schools are currently offering so many resources to mothers it is overwhelming. One education department alone offers forty-thousand worksheets and unit studies.

**Relying on worksheets and pre-packaged lesson plans is risky.** Few can be done without your involvement and all too soon you slip into slaving through fifty-six pages of busywork a day. Save worksheets on geckos and recycling etc for wet days and silly behaviour.

**Read real books on subjects that interest your children rather than little snippets of information on a worksheet.** These ticking timebombs of burnout, often come with lesson plans and the phrase LEARNING OBJECTIVES AND OUTCOMES blazoned on them somewhere. If the goal is so vague it needs to be identified with these words, it is not worth wasting energy on.

# Fighting

Fights between children are inevitable and part of them learning how to set boundaries and the consequences of breaking them. **Playing judge all day is exhausting.**

Unless it is something serious like hitting or shouting "I hate you," (where you need a bigger intervention) **make it advantageous for your children to get along by merely removing the disputed toy.**

# Ride Your Rhythms.

A woman's Energy rises and falls with her monthly cycle. Go with the flow. On high energy days, listen to the kids read and do a bit of maths. On bad days separate the kids into different rooms, give them art supplies and audiobooks to listen to.

**Get realistic about your expectations.** Many, many days you won't get any 'schoolwork' done.

| |
|---|
| **On bad days consider yourself a success if by bedtime everyone is still alive and fed (especially in the lockdown when you are all cooped up together.)** |

A crock pot is very helpful on those days. Load it up in the morning and dinner is done when you are feeling exhausted.

# Anger

**Anger and frustration are inevitable. In its horrible wake comes the feeling you hate your children. Then comes the sense of failure and guilt**. This happens to everyone, even those who start home-schooling through choice. Even the most dedicated and optimistic home-schooling mother wants to give up frequently. For you, this is not an option at the moment. It is as impossible as resigning from motherhood (and believe me, I would have quit motherhood many times if I'd found a loophole)

**Very likely as tensions rise, you will start focusing your anger on the Government for closing all the schools. While this is natural it won't help much.**

> **Your real problem is you are all out of routine and your kids are probably taking advantage of the upheaval to get very naughty.**

This will range from out-and-out rebellion (shouting, and destroying your sanity, and furniture) to a more subtle quiet disobedience that flies under your radar. Either way, you will feel loathing and hatred arise in your heart towards your children. Although these feelings are fake, they feel horribly real. **This is not the time to feel guilty, this is the time to take charge.** Now is an excellent time to download a sheet of handwriting exercises and maths sums for them to do. And if they can read and write, even a unit study with OBJECTIVES AND AIMS on it. An hour grinding through one of those will take the sting out of them. (I assure you if this is the only time they do 'real schoolwork' it will be enough because kids are not saints.)

**If you have blatant disobedience, you must find ways to make the disobedience very unpleasant for the child.**

**Under no circumstance bribe for good behaviour when a child is acting up because you are rewarding bad behaviour. Whatever you reward is what you will get plenty of.**

That goes for whining. I had a rule that if my children whined for something, they instantly did not get it. If they wanted something they had to ask respectfully.

**Disciplinary problems you have been letting slide are going to impact you, for you cannot train a child if you don't have basic obedience.** Discipline must be consistent and the rules of the home well defined. If your home is chaotic, you need to sit down and make some basic rules and start swotting up on child discipline. There is plenty of advice out there. You will find as you get disobedience under control you will stop hating your children and your home will calm into noisy-peace.

> If you are not sure whether your child is misbehaving because of naughtiness or insecurity and fear, hug him. If he is insecure or fearful, he will cling to you, if he is rebellious, he will push you away.

Tantrums are very unpleasant for you. Be creative and make sure when he throws one that it is a mutually unpleasant experience.

# The Occupational Hazard

**Unfortunately, you will go to bed most days feeling nothing got done and your children are lagging behind all the other children of the world. This will be particularly bad if you look on the internet at the fantastic things other mothers are doing with their children.**

Human nature being what it is, few women will admit they are doing worse than everyone else. Just remember when you see the fabulous violins one family made in craft lessons (this actually happened to me) most people will only publicise their best achievements. Few people will write of the horrendous day their son ate a light bulb (see my book **Eating a Light Bulb does not make you Bright.**)

I found guilt over my lack of schoolwork was worst in the twilight zone between wakefulness and sleep. At the end of the day there was always a list of things we didn't get done. Moreover, training children is a messy unproductive process.

---

**You wouldn't measure your children's physical growth on a day-to-day basis, and judging yourself day-by-day in their educational growth just as futile. By, the time your son is twenty he will be reading.**

---

# Guilt Buster

**To help combat the regular guilt, I bought a ten Column Cashbook for each of my children to record their progress.** I am not sure if you can even get them now, but some sort of spreadsheet online would do the job. At the top of each column, I wrote one or two subjects. For example, Books read aloud to child… Reading…Spelling and Grammar… Health /Social Studies… Maths… Handwriting/ Dictation… Art/ craft… Story Writing… Science… Phys-Ed.

It is surprising when you run your mind back over a disastrous home-schooling day, just how many of these boxes you can fill out with education that happened naturally. If you write them in educational jargon they look even better.

Don't make the mistake of thinking formal work is the best kind of education.

> **Pages with lots of little bitty boxes filled out make a mother feel like a 'real teacher,' but they are not the best kind of learning.**

We retain less than thirty percent of what we are taught. If we discover something for ourselves, we remember seventy percent. My children know far more than I do about computers, electricity, Latin, and science. To this day I don't know how they learnt many of the things they picked up in childhood.

# Summary

You are the lynchpin of your home, and as such, it is important to take care of your emotional wellbeing.

To counteract distress over your world spinning out of control, make an active decision to choose home-schooling.

Don't worry about your kid's socialization they will do fine.

Exhaustion is your biggest challenge so be careful how you spend your energy. Go with the flow of your body's energy rhythms and throw out anything that isn't working for you (even online schoolwork.)

Deal with rising anger and frustration by organising a basic routine and dealing with disobedient behaviour.

Have low expectations. Many days you will not get any schoolwork done (especially if your children are under ten.)

Thinking other mothers are doing better than you, and feeling guilty at the end of the day is inevitable. Soothe your conscience by recording the day's activities using educational jargon.

# Depression and Housework

**Do not underestimate how much the condition of your house will affect your mood. An ordered house makes you feel good, but a dirty, disorganized house causes depression.**

> **If you take care of the house in the morning, the house will take care of you for the rest of the day.**

If you hate housework this is another nettle you need to grasp, for in lockdown there is nowhere to escape to. It is better to create a pleasant atmosphere. If you do, you will get a great reward. This section on housework is for those of you whose house is so disorganized you don't know where to start and feel you are just shuffling things around in circles. It will take a few weeks of hard work to organize everything, but **once you get systems and good habits in place, you will be surprised how little time you have to spend each day to keep your house nice.** Best of all, you will feel much happier, and when the corona crisis passes, you will not feel ashamed when friends visit.

# If My House is in a Muddle

**If your house is in a muddle, sort it out before you start home-schooling.** Declutter drastically. If you are prone to hoarding, stop and consider what all this junk is costing you in peace-of-mind, time, and energy. **A streamlined house will go a long way to save you from burnout.**

---

**Never read a book, check emails or go online early in the morning, it is too easy to get caught up in it and the time slips away. Then for the rest of the day, you are wading through junk and being run over by chaos. Leave the computer, phone, and television off until after the jobs are done.**

---

# Toys

Children's toys are often the biggest problem. Ideally, you want to declutter when they are not around but this might be impossible. Get your husband to take them outside for a bit of physical activity or let them watch a movie in another room.

Take two black rubbish bags (they need to be black so your children can't see through them) and label them Rubbish and Donate. You will also need some large baskets or containers. If the floor of your house is a sea of toys, start in your main living room.

Move methodically across the room and as you come to an item pick it up.

Broken trucks

Legless Barbies

Junky little useless toys

Empty bottles (no matter how pretty)

Old hair barrettes, the list is endless…

Put them all in the Rubbish bag.

If the toy is good but never played with (many soft toys come into this category) put it in the 'Donate' bag.

Take three large containers and collect all the blocks of

the room and sort them into three sizes; large blocks for small children,

Medium-sized blocks for young school children

Tiny for older children.

Favourite dolls and Teddy bears, pull along toys and other things that are regularly played with go in another container.

Toys that are neither favourites nor played with can be made special by limited access to them. Put them aside in a large blanket box or cupboard for the afternoon.

I once bought a big bag of small Mc Donald Happy Meal toys from a garage sale, which I called the Sicky Toys. They only came out for unwell children when they were on the mend but still needed to stay in bed.

Warning: When your children get wind of what you are doing, a great wail will go up.

"I still play with this," shouts your son pulling a car without wheels out of the rubbish sack.

"You can't throw out Jacinda," pouts your daughter, cradling a headless doll.

"You never play with them," you say, in a defensive tone.

"Yes, we do."

"Those broken old toys have been lying behind the rubber plant for two years," you say, putting your hands on your hips.

They stare at you with a mulish expression as they hug the plastic carcasses.

Stop right there and rewind that last part. **Don't justify yourself, you are the boss of the home.** Rise to your full height, throw your shoulders back and say with confident authority:

"Choose ten toys each. For every extra toy you keep, you get one less Christmas present," you say, firing your big cannon.

This works a treat, especially in December.

"Only ten toys!" they grumble, stuffing the car and doll back into the rubbish sack.

They think ten toys is very mean. But this does not include dollhouses, bikes, Barbie families, skipping ropes, the trampoline, or the cat. And if you have four children that is still forty toys to clean up every day. **Ignore their judgmental attitudes. You don't have to jump hoops for their love, they will love you regardless, just as you love them even though they drive you crazy.**

Continue working diligently through your house until all the toys are under control.

# Clothes

**The next biggest problem area is the clothes.** The basic tools for storing clothes is dressing tables and closets. If you don't have those you need some. Generally, the smaller the person the more clothes they have. Babies are the worst offenders. **The last thing you want lying on your couch is piles of stretch-and-grows and a truckload of tee-shirts and underpants.** You know the drill now. Get out the rubbish bags and start sorting. Less is more. Although the baby and toddler will still need plenty of changes of clothing, older children do not.

> **Declutter your mind and house by simplifying your choices.**
> **Six outfits per child are twice as many clothes as your parents had when they were children.**

If you limit clothing to six outfits (not including sports gear or uniforms) you will become very selective about what you keep. I hung each outfit on one coat hanger; top, skirt, sweater, tights, and jacket etc, so they were ready to go. Then every change of season I reorganised the clothes. I threw away torn garments and stored hand-me-down clothes in the attic for the next child.

**Don't forget to deal with your own overflowing closet.** Get rid of clothes that no longer fit, are worn out, or make you feel fat.

# Socks

**Girl's tights are great because you can't lose a leg.** Avoid buying coloured socks with trains and sparkly flowers on them no matter how tempting, because every house is infested with sock snatchers. These invisible beings eat one of every pair of socks. You will waste a lot of time looking in vain for two matching socks, and your children will go around wearing blue trucks on one foot and pink unicorns on the other. **I made it a rule to only purchase navy blue socks. The sock eaters still ate them, but it wasn't so noticeable.** Moreover, I stopped squandering precious energy in futile hunts.

# Bathroom Cabinets

**Left alone for any length of time, bathroom cabinets are prolific breeders. In the cloistered darkness, an almost-empty can of shaving foam gives birth to twenty more almost-empties.** Blunt raisers, old shampoo bottles, broken combs, hairballs, and forgotten Mother's-Day-Presents multiply alarmingly. Despite the general fertility of the bathroom cabinet, some things don't increase. Cotton buds and the guts of the First-Aid kit sit like lonely islands in a grey ooze of soap scum. Now is the time to deal with them.

> **Throw open the doors of cupboards, clean all the rubbish out, and feel your mood lift.**

# The Kitchen

The refrigerator and the pantry are the big bad brothers to the bathroom cabinet. Clean them often, throw out food scraps and empty sauce bottles regularly. Open your kitchen cupboards.

**Do you really use all your kitchen appliances? Or are they like my ice cream maker and pastor machine, something you got carried away with but will never use?** If they are, put them in a box and donate them to the Salvation Army when life goes back to normal.

My oven I'm ashamed to say will probably catch on fire before I get around to cleaning it regularly. The only thing that makes this shameful habit slightly less appalling is I hate cooking and seldom bake a cake. **If you love baking and roasting, you need to be better at oven cleaning than me.**

**Clear all unnecessary clutter off your bench** so you don't have to dig out a space every time you want to make a sandwich.

**Wash the dishes after every meal.**

# Bedrooms

Once you have taken control of the toys and the clothes, the bedroom is more than half conquered. A nicely made bed improves the atmosphere of the house, which makes you feel better. **A room never looks tidy if the bed is a mess.** You will have to make the beds sometime, so make the beds early and bask in bed-endorphins for the rest of the day. Also don't neglect to open the curtains and windows to air the room out.

Despite taming the clothes and toys, two spots remain where trouble festers. **Occasionally snorkel under the bed and trawl through the closet for junk and half-eaten cheese sandwiches.**

# The lounge

> **Grandma's rule.**
> "A place for everything and everything in its place." The secret to a tidy room is clear horizontal surfaces. You can stack things vertically on shelves and the room will not look cluttered.

If you are a paper junky and have stacks of paperwork piled on the hutch-dresser and dining room table, clear them into containers and pack them away to sort out on a rainy day.

Once you have your house organized vacuuming, dusting and cleaning will become much easier and quicker. Best of all, you will feel better about your house and yourself.

# Summary

The state of your house will strongly affect your mood. If your house is chaotic it will not be a nice environment for you or your children and will cause depression. Sort out your house before attempting to home-school.

I focus in this chapter on decluttering and organizing your house so it runs smoothly; including practical advice on how to deal with the problem areas of, toys, clothes, socks, bathroom cabinets, the kitchen, bedrooms, and the lounge.

# Making a Start

## The Disastrous Start

**The old saying an ounce of practice is worth a ton of theory is true of home-schooling. It won't take long once you start home-schooling to realize much of the advice the experts are dishing out doesn't work.** We all make the mistake when we first begin home-schooling of trying to dump 'real-school' into our homes. I have had many attempts at it (usually after a long patch of getting no schoolwork done.) If you can manage it for three days you have done better than me. I only ever lasted two-and-a-half days, and the gallant attempt always followed the same pattern:

The first day starts when oestrogen is high. I am pumped up and determined I can do this, and (because of the oestrogen) the day goes not too badly. I go to bed tired but feeling I can do this.

The second day goes well enough to confirm the illusion I can do this indefinitely. Unfortunately, the chemical balance in my body tips during the night and progesterone is on the rise. Moreover, I have squandered a weeks' worth of energy in two days and I am about to pay for it big time.

I drag out of bed on Wednesday morning feeling jittery and uptight. The house is messy (I have been too busy to clean it properly) and the kids are yelling and fighting because they haven't had enough running around and free time. Disaster is imminent, yet I grit my teeth in determination.

"I WILL DO SCHOOL PROPERLY," I say, as I get out the school books.

 Attempting to get the kids motivated is like trying to keep molasses in a sieve.  Pencils drop on the floor and disappear as they dawdle through handwriting exercises. The minute my back is turned they stop all together, slumping in their seats like bananas, their dangling legs swinging in boredom.

"Sit up properly and get on with your work," I snap.

They slouch forward and scrawl sloppy letters between wide lines.

"Not that way, Hannah," I say, my voice rising, "how many times do I have to tell you to go from left to right!"

"Leave the cat alone, Marie, and get on with your work."

The baby is howling, and I forgot to load the bread-maker so lunch will be late. I shovel flour into the pot and in my haste forget the yeast.

"What's two plus two," I bark, as I feed the baby.

Blank stares.

"Come on, it's easy you should know this!"

"Eight," says Marie disinterestedly.

"Eight!" I am appalled a child of her age does not know what two plus two equals. "Why would you say eight?"

"Because eight is two circles stuck together."

That is it! The lid blows off the top of my self-control.

"Don't be such a cotton-wool head, Marie," I shout.

Now she is bawling and (ashamed of my outburst) I am close to tears myself.

I stomp out of the room only to find the toddler (making the most of my inattention) is washing all the soft toys in the toilet.

Ahhhhh!!!!!

**Surviving Home-Schooling Through the Corona Crisis**

By the time the bread is baked, school has collapsed.

"Pack away your books," I say, sawing the heavy brick of bread into slices.

When they are done, I hand my children a plate of food each.

"Go outside and play. I don't want to see you until dinner time."

The feeling is mutual.

"Yahoo," they yell, rushing off.

So ends another attempt at doing 'real-school.'

So if 'real-schooling' doesn't work, what does? Before I answer that question let's look at some of the key differences between 'real-schooling' and home-schooling.

# Difference between School and Home-Schooling

The term home-schooling is misleading. A home-school implies a school is suddenly (with much disruption) dumped into a home. To think this is as erroneous as believing a seahorse is a horse swimming in the sea; they are not even the same species. The danger of teaching your children with the same methods as a school is that burnout is inevitable; especially if your children are under ten-years-old.

> Because Home-schooling is all about training and moulding the character, home-schooling starts at birth and children learn at their own rate.

Although it varies from country to country, children

**start 'real-schools' at five** and progress year by year in grades with predetermined subjects at a speed suited to an average child.

> **The key difference between 'real-schooling' and home-schooling is 'real-schooling' educates children, while home-schooling TRAINS children. Education imparts facts, whereas training forms the mind, imparts life skills, and models patterns for children to copy.**

If your child is developing at a slower or faster rate in 'real-schools' he will be put into gifted or remedial classes. As everyone knows, there is a stigma attached to these classes. One set of children wear a badge of honour and the others a mark of shame.

The average mother values steady progress in her children over speedy progress. Most of the time I didn't even know what grade my children were supposed to be in as it wasn't important. I was, however, without any tests, painfully aware of my children's progress or lack of it.

**In 'real-school' the person with the most information (the teacher) asks questions of the people with the least information (the children) who often have little interest in the subject.**

**Children in home-schools, by contrast, pull information out of their mother on subjects that**

**spark their curiosity.** Although the approach of 'real-schools is much less effective, they have to work that way because you can't have thirty children asking questions all day. It is exhausting enough with only four children drawing information out of you. Neither can one schoolteacher cater to the interests of all the children in their care. They don't have a choice and they do the best they can. Questioning the children is an attempt to get their minds engaged with a subject the children don't care about. Unfortunately, all the questioning in the world is often not enough to spark real interest, so kids grind out busywork while boredom and frustration rise.

**'Real-schools' are a horizontal form of education. Students are segregated into flat levels by age or academic ability, thus limiting the knowledge within the group to a low ceiling.** Because of this unnatural restriction on information, the teacher's job is to introduce new ideas to expand the children's knowledge.

**Home-schools, by contrast, work vertically and children at multiple skill levels are grouped together.** Unless you have twins, all your children will be at different ages and stages of development. In large families, children can range from babies to teenagers. This vertical structure of education exposes children to a much broader range of learning opportunities. The younger children watch what the older children are doing, while older children learn basic parenting skills

**41**

as they interact with their younger siblings. It is very common to see older children reading stories to younger children or playing with the baby.

Of even more significance is the power of play. Activities like blocks, play dough, sand and water play, drawing and painting, or sports can be enjoyed in small groups of multiple ages. When this happens, **the older children will expand the younger children's world and stimulate their brains naturally.** A two-year-old's blob of play dough gains more life when his four-year-old sister plays tea parties with him. Under her tuition, he suddenly sees the blob as a birthday cake which exposes him to the concept of imagination and abstract thought.

Historically, one-on-one tuition has never been beaten by group education.

**Even in a private school with smaller classes, the ratio of students to the teacher in 'real-schools' is much higher than the number of children in a home-school.** Because of this 'Real-schools' need long hours and homework.

**Home-schools (because they are so one on one) need only twenty minutes to an-hour-and-a-half** for primary school children, while Secondary school Students can accomplish all the formal work they need to do in the morning (or less.)

'**Real-school,' needs many things;** special buildings, uniforms, a bell, desks, qualified teachers, long hours, busywork, crowd control, school buses, state funding, planning for excursions, permission slips, lunch boxes and school bags. Home-schooling needs none of these things.

**A home-school only needs an ordinary home, a library card, and a warm and responsive mother.** She doesn't have to be Mother Teresa or have endless patience. In fact, if she was a saint her children would be shocked when they met the rest of mankind. Furthermore, she will often blow her top, wonder why she ever decided to have children, and want to give up. But no matter how much her offspring drive her crazy, she keeps going because she loves them with a tenaciousness that drives her to walk over glass for them.

**In other words, home-schooling mothers are like YOU.**

# Home-Schooling the Easy Way

**In the same way that you don't have to hire a bus to go on a school trip, you don't have to imitate the clunky ways of group-education.** Why drive a clunking old car when you have a nippy Ferrari. Don't bother counting the hours that kids are at school (deducting time for recess) to get the approximate number of hours your children must slave over worksheets.

> **When you live with your kids and involve them in your life, twenty minutes for young children, up to an hour and a half for older children, does the job amply. I did even less.**

You don't have to change into a teacher. All you have to do is continue to be a warm, responsive Mum. Work with your children, discipline your children, and play with your children, in much the same way you did before they went to school.

**Throw all your childhood memories of school out and remember the way you taught your children to speak.** Chances are you don't even remember how you did it, yet without formal lessons, workbooks, or speech therapists, all your children can speak English. Some of you might even have bilingual children. You taught them by being a warm and responsive mother. When you rocked your babies, you talked to them in a baby voice and pulled exaggerated faces. You got excited when they said their first word and told all your friends about it. You decoded their sloppy attempts at words and interacted as if they were the right ones. You corrected their incorrect grammar by speaking the correct sentences back as a seamless part of the conversation. Nobody worries about teaching their children how to speak and yet the complex job gets done. You do it instinctively while you juggle other responsibilities. The same system can be applied to the foundation blocks of education.

**If you can read, write and do enough maths to know whether your bank account is in the black or the red, you have all the skills necessary to teach your children.**

> Teaching kids is not rocket science.

## The First Step to Success

**Defining goals and values are your first step.** While generally, worksheets plastered with the words 'Goals and Objectives' are another way to spell exhausted-mother, you need clearly defined goals and values.

Make your educational goals big and few, especially if your children are under ten. Reading, writing, and maths are enough as they are the foundations from which everything else flows. Values are another name for your world view, and the principles you want to pass onto your children. If you have never thought about this, now is a good time to reflect and decide what is important in life.

## The Secret to Surviving

**I know many women who like me, home-schooled for over twenty years.** We all had different temperaments and every home was unique. What worked for one woman did not work for another. **What we all had in**

**common was we increasingly focused on training, taught less, and rolled with the punches more.** Interestingly, it was the qualified school teachers who struggled the most. If they did not make the transition to more of a mothering approach, they only lasted about a year.

**Even if you hope to send your children back to school in a few months, shifting your focus to training your children rather than trying to teach 'real school' will make the experience much better for you all. You will not stress so much and your children will love it.**

That being said, it is true that even home-schoolers who primarily use the training approach do some teaching.

**But while training continues throughout the whole day, teaching only requires tiny amounts of time.** Twenty minutes to an hour and a half is plenty for primary school children (depending on their age.) If you worry about your ability to teach, just remember you are not teaching brain surgery, merely basic maths, reading, and writing. And (if you want to go fancy) a bit of science. **The homework you helped your children with every night is ample to get the job done and despite what you may fear, High School students are much easier because they direct their own learning.**

> **It is likely you will find many learning problems dissolve as kids get more freedom to explore their interests.**

But unless you are wired to love teaching (and a few mothers are) you will be exhausted after twenty minutes even if your children are not. Don't despair. There are ways to teach that don't involve your input, or at most, require a minimum of effort.

**Board games teach maths, spelling, and reading, fairly painlessly (unless it is Monopoly which always ends in fights, adults included.**

**E-books are cheap and readily available if going to the library is impossible in lockdown.**

**Audiobooks are marvellous for unskilled readers.**

**You can make small homemade books without much effort for young children.**

**For fun, you can make treasure hunts that require your kids to sound out the messages until they discover a small treat.**

**Building blocks, play dough, crayons, paper, bikes, a trampoline, sandpit, and supervised water play are fantastic basics.**

**Real stories about inspirational people like Harriet Tubman or James Cook are great. The series 'Horrible Histories' is very good both in book and DVD form.**

**Playing shops with cans from the pantry and monopoly-money teaches maths.**
**Drawing and colouring in pictures are good for creativity and fine motor skills.**

These times of self-directed learning free you up to do something you want to do. On bad days I collapsed on the couch with a cup of tea. On good days I wallpapered or quilted.

**I found the English curriculum of Letterland very helpful for teaching slow readers. It puts the complex rules of English spelling into fun stories. Even though it required my input, it was a low-stress way to teach phonics as the kids were so engaged with the stories, they badgered me to read it to them.**

# Beyond Lock down

**We won't stay shut up in our houses forever, but it is likely the reopening of schools will lag our newfound freedom.**

When this happens, feel free to interrupt your normal routine with the 'Exploring Our Environment' part of your school curriculum. Take advantage of your flexibility. You don't have to plan for weeks, sign permission slips, or hire a bus to go on a field trip.

> **If the day is beautiful, load everyone in the van and go to the beach, picnic by a lake, or take a bushwalk, if you fancy it.**

And you can go camping whenever it suits you. You don't need to stick to 'real-school' holidays. When my husband decided to go to the U.S.A for study, it was easy to move as it made no difference to our schooling. Touring the Grand Canyon, Rocky Mountains, and Niagara Falls was geography while living in another culture was social studies.

# Older Students

Most of my home-schooling friends taught more formally than me. They were much more involved and their older children spent the morning diligently working through unit studies or correspondence lessons. In the mornings their kids had school books (or laptops) open and worked away at something you would see in 'real-school.' The advantage of this method is you can recognize schooling, and you will feel secure because it looks like the teaching you know. The disadvantage is it ties up your time.

If like me, you don't like formal teaching and you have tons of other things you would rather do, (including working from home) there is a much easier way to get the job done.

In this more relaxed system, you are not a 'teacher' you are an empowerer.

## This is how you do it.

Television, movies and electronic games are only for the evenings. Everyone in the family gets a library card and works hard in the morning to get the household chores out of the way. Then everyone (including you) has large chunks of unscheduled time to explore the things they are fascinated with.

When you first implement your new system, your children will complain of boredom. Do not panic, boredom will not kill them. Boredom is an unpleasant yet fabulous emotion. It is the springboard of creativity. You will feel the benefit of it yourself as the lockdown progresses. Those jobs you have been putting off, and the book you've been planning to write will suddenly get done.

Cheerfully say to your whinging offspring:

"The house, garage, and back yard are bursting with things to do. Draw a picture or play a board game or something."

They will show you what they think of these lame ideas by pulling a face and lolling on the kitchen floor with their legs on the cupboard doors. Ignore their judgemental attitude and get on with what you want to do. Eventually, they will get off the floor and trail behind you grizzling:

"I'm borrrred."

Continue to hold your nerve. The sentence, "I'm borrrred," is brother to "I'm hungrrry."

Just as the hungrrry child is not hungry enough to chow down a carrot, a borrred child is not bored enough to sweep the floor. In both cases, they are hoping you are a magician about to pull a treat out of the hat.

"Don't worry, I have plenty of jobs for everyone who is bored," you say. "The toilet needs extra cleaning."

Once they realise your hat is full of broccoli and toilets, not the chips and movie they expected, they will stop badgering you. As they stomp off in disgust, call after them:

"Anyone who has not found something constructive to do within the next five minutes gets a job."

The stomping turns into running as your kids rush to get a game out of the cupboard.

**Of course, it is Monopoly, which is fabulous for maths but always ends in fighting and tears. You continue working until the inevitable ruckus happens. Then you intervene with a downloaded worksheet.**

**"Betty, I want half a page of handwriting done," you say, handing a worksheet to your five-year-old. "Tom, you can do a page of maths. Ask Sally for help if you get stuck with the long division. Sally, write me a story about a dog that runs away. If you don't know how to spell a word, sound it out. If I hear any silly talk or fighting, you will have to weed the garden when you have finished."**

**The kids settle down as they grind through their schoolwork.**

Once your children realize you will leave them alone when they are doing something constructive, they will start finding interesting things to do. When this happens, real learning escalates.

Your home-school won't look anything like 'real-school' it will look like hobbies on steroids. While this kind of learning does not follow a prescribed curriculum, it is rich. All you have to do is stay near enough to [1]monitor the noises and pull in the resources your kids need but can't get for themselves. I took them

1    See Monitoring the Noises in 'Your Home-schooling Toolkit'

to the library, provided tables for roadside stalls, bought a skeleton, and set up a shop in the front room of my house, among other things. They drew and wrote stories, made electrical gizmos, rode horses, built tree huts, sewed, and sold flowers at the gate, etc. Meanwhile, I supervised as I wallpapered and painted.

**I even worked on Friday mornings in the antique shop next door by using this system.** Of course, all of my children were over ten by then. If they were younger, I wouldn't have dreamed of attempting it. My house had a wooden floor and I could hear if they were running around inside. The minute my house sounded like a drum I phoned them and gave them schoolwork assignments, or popped my head above the fence and dispensed jobs.

# The Downside

**The only downside to this fabulous system is you have to be brave enough to let go of convention and trust the kids are learning.**

This is a struggle for those of us steeped in 'real-school' from birth because we are conditioned to believe learning is formal and arduous. Although children under this system will learn magnificently, it is not showy and the mother who takes this path will not have the pleasure of feeling she is a good teacher. She can, however, still enjoy the feeling of being a good mother.

I counteracted this by recording the day's activities in my column cash books. Furthermore, I read up on child development and how the brain works.

**The most helpful resource I found was research by Raymond and Dorothy Moore.** The late Raymond and Dorothy Moore are known as the grandparents of home-schooling. Raymond Moore was a professional in the field of education. He was a classroom teacher and administrator and worked in public schools and universities. His wife Dorothy was a reading specialist. Together they conducted extensive research into the effects of early formal education on children. The Moores concluded after thirty years of research, that equal measures of manual labour, schoolwork, and acts of service, in the environment of a loving home were the best form of education for children under ten.

They wrote many books on home-schooling including 'Better Late Than Early' which I highly recommend if you have a late-blooming child.

---

**Trying to home-school like a school, is like trying to squeeze a cathedral's pipe organ into a tiny-house.**

---

# Summary

Home-schooling is not a school in the home, there are many fundamental differences, including the children to adult ratio, and age ranges. The primary difference, however, is schools educate children from age five and home-schools train children from birth.

You don't have to become a mini-school, it is not the most effective way to teach. Instead, continue teaching the way you taught your children to speak.

Define your goals and values before you start so you know where you are heading. Make them few and big. Stick to reading, writing, and maths if your children are under five. If you don't know what values are important, now is a good time to think about them.

Once the lockdown is over, take holidays and day trips when you want to.

Become an empowerer rather than a teacher. The easiest way of home-schooling is to just live with your children and get them to help with the household chores. Ban electronic entertainment during the day and let boredom arise. Have plenty of books, board games, and art supplies available. Tell them to find something to do. Leave them alone when they are doing something constructive. Intervene with jobs or worksheets when they fight or get silly.

The downside of the system is it won't look like schoolwork and you will feel guilty. Counteract it with recording the day's activities and swot up on the brain and how learning really happens.

Raymond and Dorothy Moore were pioneers of home-schooling. They researched home-schoolers for thirty years. Their books are a helpful resource.

# Home-Schooling Toolkit

## The Golden Tool

Chores and acts of service are the golden tools of your home-schooling toolkit. Chores train diligence, obedience, and life skills. Acts of service train kindness and good character.

**After feeding everyone get on to the housework smartly. And not just you. Housework is a prime tool for training the character.** As a mother, your job is so much more than just education. A clever man or woman who knows a lot but cannot finish anything and has no concern for others is not the result you are aiming for.

> Many days you will not have the energy to both train the character and teach reading. On those days, choose character over education.

If it takes you all morning to repeatedly put Johnny in the naughty corner because he won't dust the hall table, keep at it until he does. The issue here is pecking order, not housework. You will probably be so exhausted by the end of the tussle you have to have an afternoon sleep. (Something I highly recommend).

> Many days you will not get any school work done. Don't despair, the years will know what the days never know, your children will end up literate by the time they are adults even if they currently trail their peers.

**Train your children to make their beds from an early age.** If a child is not helping, he will be wrecking the house as you tidy. Now you are home-schooling you do not have the luxury of doing it all yourself. Yes, it will initially take three times longer, but in the long term, it will pay big dividends, as you will have to do less and less as your children learn to be good workers.

I had four clean-up times during the day. The biggest clean-up was immediately after breakfast. Smaller clean-ups happened after lunch, before dinner, and once the kids were in bed.

I divided the jobs into:

Bed making

Washing, drying and putting away the dishes

Dusting

Cleaning the handbasin

Cleaning the toilet

Setting and clearing the table

Hanging out the washing

Bringing in the washing

Folding the washing.

Putting the washing away

I divided these jobs among the children and rotated them. My job was to oversee and fix up the sloppy finish.

# Rewards and Incentives

Take strict control of the television and video games. Movies and games can be used as rewards at the end of the day.

**Never have the television blaring in the background (especially in the morning.) You don't need the**

**extra din or distraction. You are not babysitting your children you are training them.** Forbid turning the television on without permission and if you have repeated flouting of your law, remove it altogether. Several weeks with nothing will make them very respectful when you bring it back. **If phones and other electronic devices give you trouble, confiscate them for a while.** If your child fusses over this, the more he argues, the longer he loses the item.

**Draw up a chores roster and rotate the jobs.** A system of gold stars to reward jobs well done is popular with younger children. A small prize for ten stars is an added incentive.

**If you can afford to pay your children small sums of money for extra jobs** like gardening, sweeping the path, washing down the house, etc. This will give them the incentive to work hard. Moreover, if they have a little cash in their pocket you have the leverage of fines to help limit bad behaviour.

While I found workbooks were not much good for real teaching, they are great for the child who loves filling in boxes. I used them as a reward for children having acquired the skills needed to complete them. Maths workbooks with pictures and stickers for sticking on strategic spots were especially popular with my second child.

# Watchful Neglect

Watchful neglect is a phrase I think my mother might have coined.

> Watchful neglect is the art of remaining in the background fully aware of what is going on yet appearing to see nothing.

It is the complete opposite of the helicopter parent who hovers about anxiously. Watchful neglect is easy on you because you can get on with something else while you monitor the safety of your kids. Small children need constant watching, but they enjoy a measure of independence and freedom when you employ watchful neglect. You don't have to pretend not to see them, all you need is an activity you want to get on with yourself.

> A grazing horse with a playful foal is a wonderful example of watchful neglect.

The foal will not wander far and will often check in with its mother. Watchful neglect for young children is always done within eye range. As children get older, you can extend your surveillance range by monitoring the noises.

# Monitor the Noises in Your Home

> Monitoring the Noises is long-distance Watchful Neglect and used for older children.

**If I was in a different room or the children were outside, I monitored the quality of their activity by the noise level.** If there was a low drone like a healthy hive, I left everyone alone to pursue their interests. But if the noise escalated into the raucous laughing of hyenas I intervened, (sometimes unpleasantly) because from hyenas it was a small step to tears and fighting.

If you listen you will easily hear when your bumblebees change into hyenas. The moment you hear it, stop what you are doing and tell everyone involved in the ruckus to pack away all the board games and activities. Now is a great time to download some of those forty-thousand worksheets at your disposal. Half an hour of handwriting, maths, or spelling should be enough to turn the hyenas back into bumblebees. For children who can read and write, a worksheet with LEARNING GOALS AND OBJECTIVES blazed over it should do the trick.

# A Teachable Moment

A teachable moment is a golden moment. It is when your child's mind is as receptive as a sponge; the complete opposite to the concrete pad the times-tables usually hit. Things like getting a new bike, finding a lizard, or the cat dying, spark a teachable moment. Unless you are rushing to the hospital, seize a teachable moment, it is a brief opportunity to impart ideas and values swiftly and easily.

# Summary

Chores and acts of service are a powerful tool for training your children. Many days you will not have the energy to both train the character and do schoolwork. If you have to choose, character training is the best choice in the long run.

Train your children to work from an early age. Housework is good for building character, teaching obedience, and eventually lightens your workload. I had four clean-ups during the day; one big one straight after breakfast, and three smaller ones after meals and before dinner.

Divide the regular jobs and rotate them.

Rewards and incentives are useful for increasing motivation. Charts and stars and small prizes for ten stars earned are one way of rewarding work.

The tools of Watchful Neglect and Monitoring the

Noises, free children to get on with activities in an atmosphere of minimal supervision. Watchful Neglect is best demonstrated by a grazing mare with a playful foal. Monitoring the Noises is longer range supervision for older children. It is accomplished by listening and intervening when constructive humming changes into fighting and silliness.

The teachable moment is when a child is highly interested in something. It is usually triggered by something and can happen at any moment. Flow with it if you possibly can, it is your best opportunity to pass on knowledge or values.

# Your Needs

## What About Your Needs?

Children are absorbing if you allow them to be. You need some enthralling hobby or work that makes you excited to get up in the morning.

I love my husband and my children but they are not what makes me bounce out of bed excited to start a new day. In my home-schooling days, it was quilting, cross-stitching and renovating my old house. So many of the things a woman does each day have to be done all over again the next day, and the next, and the next... There is no progress in these jobs, just an endless round of maintenance. Children, on the other hand, do progress. But the progress is too long term for any immediate gratification. Some parents get around this by competing through their children.

> Competing through children is a destructive game whether you win or lose and best avoided at all costs.

**The feeling of progress is very good for the soul. You need something that at the end of the day you can look at and feel you have made progress.** There are many things you can do in the home that will give you that feeling. Most women like crafts of some sort and crafts drip with endorphins. A sewing machine is very useful and not that hard to use. A bit of practice can save you heaps of money on curtains, which are simple to make. Also, scrapbooking, writing, gardening, preserving, cooking, embroidery, music, and online studies are just a few interests that can be indulged in.

**The trick to it is it must be something flexible that can be picked up and put down easily because you won't get long patches of uninterrupted time.**

# Time for You

> Regardless of how long you home-school, you must run it like a marathon, not a sprint if you want to avoid burnout.

**Carve out time for yourself, especially if you have been used to the kids out of the house for six hours a day.**

**I had a box of special toys that only came out in the**

**afternoon.** After lunch from 1-3 pm the children chose a special toy, a story tape, and some sort of afternoon activity from the box. Then I sent each child to a separate room (to stop fighting and silliness) That was my break.

**Furthermore, every couple of months my husband took over for the weekend and I went away for a complete break.**

In lockdown, this won't be possible but your husband or even an older child (bribed) might be able to relieve you of many jobs occasionally, so you can have a reprieve for a day every so often.

# Home Businesses

**Home businesses (especially online ones) are possible to run alongside home-schooling, especially if your children are older. Older children can even help you out in a family-run business.**

If your children are under ten, you can still do things. The trick, however, is your work and projects have to be poked into gaps when you have energy and must take second place to the kids, as it is disastrous to do it the other way around.

**The woman who manages to float a small business while home-schooling gains a great reward. It provides her with a sense of accomplishment and boosts the family income a little.**

**Moreover, as motherhood primarily revolves around the needs of others, it gives her a sense of identity and something to build on when she empty nests.**

A word of caution. If you have a high-powered job that requires intense concentration, I suggest you put it on hold until your children go back to school because children, twenty-four-hours a day seven days a week, is exhausting, and it is essential you are not too distracted to supervise properly.

# Summary

Do something for yourself. A woman's work is repetitive and without short-term gratification. Hobbies make the day exciting. Crafts and online study, or even a home business, are ideal.

The key to success is your interests must be flexible and worked around the needs of the children. This is especially true if your children are under ten. Put a high-powered job on hold until the kids go back to school.

Carve out recovery time for yourself. Put the children in separate rooms in the afternoon with special toys and activities to keep them occupied while you have a sleep or have free time.

Do your best to get a complete break occasionally. If you can't get the weekend off, your husband or older children could take over your duties for a day.

# Children's Needs

## Birth to Crawling

**The baby's greatest need is loving continuous care by one or two parents.** In addition to his physical needs, he needs cuddling, smiling conversation, and rocking. Within reason, his feeding, bath time, play and bedtime should come at about the same time each day to help build a sense of order and security.

**The home does not have to be quiet for a baby to sleep. He will sleep through all sorts of noise if it is part of the normal background of your home.**

## Useful tools to stimulate his brain are:

Mobiles hanging from his cot.

A baby gym he can lie under and look at interesting things.

Rattles, teething rings, and plastic keys.

A bouncer net is great for him and even better for you. They free up your hands as you can rock him with your foot.

A walker frame with a tray is great for sitting babies.

As is a jolly jumper. Babies love those things and are hilarious the way they bounce and leap about in them.

Don't leave the baby out when you read to your older children. Hold them on your lap or bundle them in the middle of the group at storytime.

> **Older children are a great resource. They can help in many ways. Don't be tempted to overuse them, however, they need their childhood.**
> **The burden of raising children belongs to you.**

# Crawlers

**The floor of the lounge of a typical home-school is a minefield for a crawling baby.**

Much of the day the floor is a sea of islands. One island is Lego blocks while train tracks circle another island, the coffee table is covered in colouring-in books, while little bitty furniture lies scattered all round a doll's house. As you well know, a crawler will swallow the small blocks, eat crayons, derail the train, and poke his eye out with a chair if he gets the chance. He is also a right pain, capable of wrecking treasures. Keep him away from card castles and the worlds-longest-domino-chain with a playpen. He can sit in his private island in the middle of the activity and feel part of the family. In his pen, he can have big blocks with rounded edges, a big ball, soft toys and board books. Before long he will be invited to play the unpopular part of the baby in a game of mothers and fathers.

> He will not come to harm zooming around the room in a plastic ladybird pram wearing reindeer-antlers, because you are monitoring the situation with watchful neglect.

# Toddlers

> Don't bother buying Christmas presents for a toddler if you are strapped for cash for he will be more delighted with the coloured paper around the toy than the toy.

**A love affair with cardboard boxes starts at this age and continues for many years.** A one-year-old will be delighted with a humble banana box. Once he gets to the sophisticated age of six, however, you have to produce a refrigerator box to get the same reaction.

**The pot cupboard is a traditional favourite.** Adam and Eve's children would have played with their mother's cooking pots and spoons. Different sizes are good for stacking and make Baby's first drum kit. Sandpits, buckets and spades, water toys, measuring cups, mud, and a ride-on-scooter are gold star toys, as are push-and-pull toys and little wagons.

## Recipe for Playdough

2 cups of flour

Half a cup of oil

Food colouring

-------------

1 Add the oil to the flour and mix

2 Add food colouring

3 Add and mix in enough water to make a soft dough

4 Kneed it until it is smooth

Keep it in the fridge and you can use it over and over. Make sure you label it so your husband won't scoff it down by accident.

**If you are locked up in an apartment with small children during the lockdown, you are in a difficult situation.**

A small exercise trampoline could help run steam off your children. A small table and chair set and play dough is another perennial goodie. On the days you can stand it, he will enjoy finger painting.

While the toddler is becoming more socially aware and enjoys interactions with his older siblings, he is of course exceedingly self-absorbed.

It is your job for the next twenty-years to teach him the astonishing fact that while he is very valuable, the universe does not actually revolve around him.

**This is a long hard job and you need to start as soon as he can walk.** Although it is difficult to believe you are on the same team, your other children will accidentally help you with this job. Like pebbles rumbling back and forth on a beach, they will knock the sharp bits off each other. Or perhaps more realistically, at least point out (in breath-taking truthfulness) one another's faults.

At this age, your child is also becoming aware of pecking order.

---

**The toddler passionately wants to know if you are a worthy leader and will test you to see if you are. Expect many battles.**

---

Giving in for the sake of peace is short-sighted. If you ask him to pick up a block and he resists, he has declared war. Don't disappoint him. Continue insisting he picks it up until he does.

**If he picks a battle just as you are about to listen to reading, forget the reading and deal with him.**

---

**Because you must insist on having your commands obeyed, be careful to ask only for things a toddler is capable of doing**

---

# Three to Five-Year-olds

**Three to five-year-olds may have outgrown the pot cupboard, but most of the gold star toys remain favourites.**

Pre-schoolers still enjoy sand-pits, play dough, and water play. Ride-on-scooters are upgraded to tricycles.

**Scribbles are evolving into rudimentary pictures on drawing pads and the wallpaper behind the bedroom curtains.**

The vocabulary of some chatterboxes may be surprisingly advanced by three. But the mothers of these children are more likely to groan over their youngster's accomplishment than preen themselves.

> **While it is popular to start teaching a child the alphabet and numbers during this time, training in basic obedience is a better use of your energy as it is the foundation block of learning.**

Besides, it is likely the older kids are raucously singing the alphabet song and yelling out numbers as they move along board games. The trickle-down effect of this ends up coating him with pre-reading and maths skills. That goes for colours too. Way back in the forgotten days when your first child was three, I'm sure you spent time teaching your little chickadee the colours.

**Don't waste your time on colours now you are home-schooling multiple children.**

Kids pick that kind of stuff up by themselves and the older children will probably teach them by accident.

**Even three-year-olds like crafts.** Egg boxes, glue, coloured paper, wood offcuts, cardboard, paint and ice cream containers are some of the things they could use.

**Dress-up clothes are good for the imagination and your sanity on wet days.** As is the clothes horse; draped with blankets it is a hut.

**Board books are replaced with picture books** that have lots of interesting things for children to look at. Your regular story time can be boosted with audiobooks.

# Five to Seven

**ALERT STATIONS, the child is five. Suddenly there is pressure on him to perform to certain standards. Or rather, there was until coronavirus blew everything apart.**

**You may have been thrust into the world of home-schooling unwillingly, but at least the pressure to perform is off.** Despite the overwhelming number of worksheets available, everything is so chaotic nobody is really expecting you to do much more than keep your children safe, fed, and off the streets.

So relax, twenty minutes on your good days will be more than enough. Focus on reading, writing, and maths, for they are the basic building blocks of education.

**Schoolwork is not the place do battle over obedience. You can't be sure if you are dealing with disobedience, a learning difficulty, or lack of readiness. If you suspect you are dealing with rebellion, stop the schoolwork and start the child on simple chores that you know he can do. The jobs will immediately sort out the difference.**

**Teach counting and number recognition;** one to ten to begin with, and when they have mastered that, ten to twenty. Get them counting blocks, dried beans, and other objects, and do simple addition and subtraction with them. Sort candy into different colours, and once they have done it reward them with a peice. Board games are very useful. Games like Snakes and Ladders and dominoes sneak maths into children's minds like fish wrapped around the cat's worm-pill.

**Teach the sounds of the alphabet letters, not their names.** The sounds of letters are very important while the names are not. Don't clutter their minds with unimportant trivia. In due time they will pick up the official names.

**Now is when you will regret calling your child a Welsh name twenty letters long because you'll have to teach him how to write it;** and not with all uppercase letters. Spell Llandfairpwllgwyngull Bloggs with a capital L and B while the rest of the letters are lower case.

**The curriculum Letterland by Lyn Wendon and used in many British schools is very good.** It teaches with stories and pictures and is helpful for children who struggle in this area. 'First Steps in Letterland ' lays the foundation of basic phonics while 'Big Strides in Letterland,' deals with more advanced phonics.

**You can stick words like chair and table on chairs and tables** for a week every so often. This is a passive form of flashcards. Don't leave them too long. They are ugly and you don't want them to become so familiar nobody sees them anymore.

**Audiobooks with physical books to read along with them are great** for beginner readers. As are easily memorized books like Dr Seuss.

**Make use of a few of those forty-thousand worksheets** available to you and download handwriting worksheets. Pick the prettiest ones with wide lines that look like a two-lane road with the centre line dotted in. Show your child how to hold the pencil properly, then put your hand over their hand and guide them through the proper letter formation. Talking as you go through each circuit, e.g.

"Little A, start at the top, slide down and around and back up again in a big circle and then slide down the stalk at the side."

After forming a few letters with them, get them to have a go by themselves. Don't expect to keep this up for long. Ten minutes will leave you feeling like a truck has run over you. Don't forget to add a few numbers each time.

**Use flashcards and teach family groups of words,** e.g. run, running, runner, rerun or rhyming words.

If reading and spelling are very difficult for your child, just do your best.

> **Dyslexia is riddled through my extended family and reading and spelling were a huge struggle for some of my kids. My highly dyslexic son, who I despaired over teaching to read, was (without special intervention) reading by twenty and passionate about books by twenty-two.**

**Science at this age is like a bell on a bicycle, fancy but not necessary.** If you disagree, cut the top off a carrot and put it in a saucer of water on the windowsill so the kids can watch it grow. Bean sprouts are also a possibility.

The sandpit and water play remain popular. Now that he does not automatically eat everything, plasticine can extend the play dough experience and help develop fine motor skills. Likewise, the tricycle can upgrade to a bicycle with trainer wheels. A trampoline is an excellent tool, as are swings and a tree hut (if your husband is into slapping a platform in the oak tree out the back.)

**For you sporty families** whose babies could roll a ball before they could walk, balls and bats will be increasingly important. Because of the corona scare, team sports will not be possible at the moment. But that won't stop you from playing games in your yard.

**Art and crafts can be extended into woodwork with small hammers and saws.** Unfortunately, some of your children will be more proficient with these than you will like.

> Our deck was chewed around the edges before
> we realized what our son was doing with his new
> saw. Watch out for nails also. The same boy nailed
> a whole box of them into the back lawn. The
> lawnmower was never the same after my husband
> ran over them.

If you can stand the smell and big licky tongue of a
dog, and don't mind when the kids sneak it into their
beds, the family dog is the ultimate toy. Downgrade to
a cat if you want a less smelly and lower maintenance
model. A fish is a lame substitute for either, but better
than nothing if you are in an apartment that won't let
you keep pets.

# Seven to Twelve

**As kids grow work is increasingly important and
they need increasing amounts of it.** Gardening,
sweeping the path, lawn mowing can be added to your
basic list. Even a kid slow at maths will be quick to
grasp the value of numbers if it is linked to money. You
could think about paying him small amounts of money
for extra jobs.

**Keep on building those basic foundation blocks of
reading, writing and arithmetic. By now there is a
huge gap between early and late developers.** Some
kids will be fluent in reading while others are struggling

to read 'the cat sat on the mat.' Hold onto your courage and keep at it (in a relaxed way) if your child is trailing. So long as he is engaged with life and eager to try things that interest him don't panic.

---

**I know a home-schooling family who spent most of their time twisting themselves into knots and doing acrobatics.**

---

Among the kids of the home-schooling support group, these children were shining stars. The small fry gathered around them and cried:

"Walk on your hands, and do a flip, Andrew, twist your foot over your head, Jillian."

Like my kids, they trailed their peers in the three Rs. But all of them ended up literate by the time they were adults.

As children age from seven through to twelve, the constructive debris spread over your lounge floor and along the veranda will gradually evolve from soft toys and colouring books to soldering irons, and computer carcasses, or things of an equally ugly nature. Your job will also evolve from Teacher to Chief Purchasing Officer and head of Customer Support as you empower their pursuit of fascinating subjects.

> Towards the end of these years, my girls got horses and my son developed the Girl-Booby-Trap using an electric fence. Like all new inventions it had teething problems, he and his brother were the only ones who ended up getting zapped.

Nine is considered a good age to start children on a musical instrument. We started all the kids on the recorder when they were this age because lessons were cheap and recorders cost nine-dollars-ninety-five-cents. After a couple of years, the girls graduated to sawing away on violins. It was pretty bad. Their father (who should have been more saintly) banned them from practising when he was home. He also insisted on the same rule when Marie got passionate about listening to opera.

# High School Students

**High School students are much easier than primary school students** simply because they are older and usually can read. Even super late bloomers (whose reading and spelling are sketchy) are resourceful at digging out information on the subjects they are passionate about. By now their personalities and interests are more pronounced and they can do more interesting stuff.

**When my eldest daughter was fourteen, she volunteered to work in a florist** of some friends of mine. For the next three years, she worked in two florists and became fully trained. Although she decided to become a writer and illustrator instead, the skills she learned during those years are very useful. She can go into a mediocre garden and pluck a professional bouquet out of it.

**And as for all the violin lessons, the dreadful fighting cat noises eventually turned into passable fiddle music.** Towards the end of the High School years, we joined together with another home-schooling family and formed a Celtic band. For a couple of years, we ran dances in quaint country halls, which was fun.

For those of you who are into sport big time, you will be aware I write little about sport. That is because we are not a sporty family. This is one of the great things of home-schooling: **Families can build their own special identity.**

Home-schooling families who were sporty spent large amounts of their time on sports fields or horses.

---

**If schools start ramping up the pressure with long distance education, all the mothers of the world will cry out in anger because five hours of schoolwork is not practical.**

---

# Summary

Babies need loving and continuous care from one or two parents. Make sure they get plenty of sleep and stimulate their brains by talking to them, cuddling, and providing bright things for them to look at.

Protect crawlers from small toys littered about and stop them from destroying older children's projects. Older children will help stimulate their brains by playing with them. Toys suitable for sucking and chewing are useful.

Toddlers love simple things best. Boxes, paper and the pot cupboard. Premium activities both now and for years to come include, sand and water, things to ride, jump, and swing on, a small table and play dough.

Sports and games are good for big body movement and kids of all ages like crafts.

Teach the basics of reading, writing, and maths as children show signs of readiness. Twenty minutes a day are enough.

Children take on more responsibility for their education as they get older, and physical labour and chores are increasingly important. If you have the opportunity, extend a child's interest by voluntary work in the community or a small paid job.

# Other Issues

## The Late-Bloomer

> The mother of late-blooming kids feels she is a worse teacher than the mother of early bloomers.

Mothers of early bloomers are likely to boast:

"My Susan has just turned three and already she is reading the wall street journal."

If your children are trailing Susan by many years don't despair. **Production lines and quality control is great for industry but terrible for kids.** Kids come in all shapes, sizes, growth spurts, talents and interests. One size of education does not fit all. Home-schooling may be the best thing that could happen for some of your children. Children are natural learning machines if they are encouraged to follow their interests and explore their environment. An ability to spout off a narrow band of facts does not translate into a lifelong interest in learning. The home is an ideal place to foster the mind.

> **Raymond and Dorothy Moore tracked home-schooling students in a thirty-year-study and found that everything students learn throughout their school life can be learnt in three years if they start much later.**

**If you have a late bloomer, the most important thing you can do is let the child go at his own pace and protect both his and your belief that he can learn.** Do your best not to look at what their peers are accomplishing, it will throw you into a tailspin. Birthdays are the worst. Two of my children were very late bloomers and slow to read. Every year as we blew out the candles on the cake, I panicked over their progress.

My daughter struggled to read early readers until she was nearly ten. Then overnight (literally) she could suddenly read full-sized adventure storybooks with no pictures. It was like the miracle of the blind man who could suddenly see.

"What happened?" I asked her, as we jumped around the room for joy.

"I dunno, I just looked at the page and suddenly I could read. Hannah learns in steps and stairs, but I learn in swirls."

How true. **A swirly learner has a bazar learning style.** If they are not interested in a subject it is almost impossible to teach them. Then when you least expect it, they do something amazing.

**They are very bright (even gifted) children who often seem stupid. Probably Albert Einstein was a swirly learner.**

Did all the frustrating reading lessons help or hinder my swirly learner? Did they suddenly bear fruit or would she have picked reading up without my help the same way she taught herself Latin? I don't know. All I know is one day she was unable to read and the next day she could.

I have read about this phenomenon. While it is not common, it is common enough for someone to write about it. A friend of mine had a son who did the same thing at twelve. I hoped my other late bloomer might have a miraculous reading swirl, but he never did.

"My brain came like a kit set from America," said Marie, "But Mark's brain is on a slow boat from China."

Once again, my daughter pegged it.

**Mark was so late blooming he would have been in remedial classes in everything if he had gone to 'real-school.'** His father who had the same learning style came out of school convinced he was dumb, yet he went on to earn two Masters degrees in science. Eventually, Mark, (who seldom realized he trailed his peers and spent most of his childhood playing with Lego) caught up without drama. It took him until he was twenty to read properly and two more years to get passionate about books.

**There have been no swirls for Mark. He was a bud opening ever so slowly into a magnificent bloom.**

Mark's physical body has mirrored the process of his mind. He was a weedy, scrappy little kid. His head looked too big for his little skinny arms and legs and he had a pronounced lisp. The lisp bothered me because all my other children were clear speakers and talked like dictionaries. My father suggested I put him in speech therapy but I felt at a gut level it was only immaturity and he would grow out of it.

Today there is no trace of his lisp. Moreover, in his late teens, he had an enormous growth spurt and now is a tall and strongly built man. He spent most of his tenth year standing behind his older brother, watching him as he worked on the computer. This started Mark's love affair with the computer.

At age eleven he was tapping away on an old computer himself. When his brother suggested he try 3D modelling using the program, Blender, he was hooked. From then on, he spent all his time on the computer. I got technical books out of the library and we sat side by side on the couch like Jack Sprat and his wife; I could read yet understood nothing I was reading, while, Mark, who could not read, understood everything I read. Between these books, podcasts and online tutorials, Mark taught himself computer animation, his reading skills slowly improving as he explored his passion.

He is currently enrolled at University in his third year of Computer Science. He is a keen, self-motivated learner and doing so well it makes all my past fears (and secret tears) seem ludicrous.

So, if your child is mucking around and the three Rs don't seem to be happening, don't despair, you probably have a late bloomer or a swirly learner, just make sure they are doing something constructive that they love.

# Teenage boys

**There is no doubt about it, teenage boys can be a huge challenge.** Testosterone is kicking in and they can be very troublesome. Physical work is the best cure, if possible. If you have a large yard think about getting him to dig it into a big garden. Or maybe a hole for a deep swimming pool?

---

**There is something about digging that settles boys down.**

---

The normal routine of schoolwork in the morning is better swapped around once boys become difficult. For maximum benefit, **physical labour is best performed in the morning as testosterone is at its height in the morning** and diminishes as the day progresses. If you can't get him digging, you can have the cleanest house in the neighbourhood. Get him washing it down, water-blast the paths, mow the lawn, clean the deck, clean out the pantry, etc. He will, of course, be very resistant.

**If you can afford to pay him something it will help sweeten his attitude.**

Hopefully, he is not accustomed to getting a lot of pocket money for doing nothing. If he is, now is a good time to educate him about the real world. If you can't afford money, be creative and think up privileges or something he might like. Keep in mind (if he gets stroppy over his new routine) this is the one time he cannot rush off to his friends or down the road, so use that to your advantage.

My second son was not a problem, but my eldest son is a high-powered individual. If I did not work him in the morning, by afternoon he was argumentative and disruptive. I paid him ten dollars for a morning's worth of work. Once he had had two hours of digging, he was happy to work away at school work in the afternoon. Because we had thirty acres, I also got him fencing and landscaping and he turned into a great asset. He developed problem-solving skills and during the day when his father was at work, I was able to rely on him to get the van out of a bog or fix a leaking tap. On the days I ran out of ideas I got him digging up more garden. We had a huge potato patch the year he was fifteen.

As he matured and grew in responsibility, he concluded at about age sixteen that I was a terrible teacher and he needed to take control of his own education. This should be the goal of every home-schooling mum, as once a child realizes this, he is on the path to lifelong learning,

That he was used to taking responsibility for his education helped him hugely in his transition to university. He attended University and was on the Deans Merit List four years running. He graduated in 2019 with First Class Honours in Electrical Engineering.

# The Policeman child

Most children will love a more relaxed education. But some of you might have a policeman child. I never had a policeman child, but one of my friends did.

**The policeman child is a child who loves workbooks and worksheets.** This in itself is not a problem. By all means, download all the worksheets and unit studies she desires.

**The trouble comes when this child thinks the rest of**

**the family should be doing proper 'real-school.'**

Moreover, this bossy individual will get on your case and expect you to get your act together and spoon-feed her and her siblings like a 'real teacher.' While most children do not need de-schooling when 'real-school' stops (they take to it like a duck to water) a policeman-child who gains a sense of accomplishment by jumping through hoops might struggle with this.

Do not let this child turn your home into a pseudo 'real-school.' The other kids will hate it and you will burn out. Moreover, a child who calls the shots will shoulder a sense of responsibility for the education of the whole family. This is a heavy load even for you. She needs to be protected from this weight.

> **Whatever it takes, let her know you are the boss. Regardless of how inadequate you feel, speak confidently and take the lead.**

Find some online study for her and print her out certificates of achievement when she has finished a unit study. When she starts to insist all her siblings have to do the same thing, tell her to mind her own business and stop being a busybody.

# Summary

**Children develop at differing rates.** By age five there is a huge difference between early and late-bloomers. Let late-bloomers go at their own pace, they will eventually read and write. Progress is more important than speed. It is vital you protect their belief in themselves that they can learn. As much as possible shield them from unfavourable comparisons.

**Swirly learners have a bazar learning style.** They are gifted children who often look stupid. They have a global way of processing which takes longer initially. These children often 'miraculously' go from stumbling over an early reader one day to reading a novel the next. It is freaky when it happens.

**Teenage boys can be difficult.** Swap their routine to physical labour in the morning when testosterone is high to settle them down. Then they can do schoolwork in the afternoon. Things improve when they take responsibility for their education. This often happens somewhere around age fifteen or sixteen. Once this happens learning escalates.

**The Policeman child loves worksheets and workbooks.** This is a good thing. She probably is a gifted administrator. Download as many lesson plans as she wants. The trouble comes when she thinks the rest of the family must 'real-school.' Don't let a policeman child boss you around and usurp your role as the educational head of the home

---

If a teacher with a classroom of twenty children tries to give children individual attention, each child gets three minutes an hour. Twenty minutes of home-schooling is worth more than five hours of school.

---

# Pulling It All Together

## What a Typical Home-Schooling Day Might Look Like

> Train your children to stay in bed
>
> until you let them up.

**6:00** The baby wakes up. You change him, take him back to bed and breast-feed him.

**6:15** Get up, put the baby back to bed, and have breakfast with your husband before he goes to work. (One of the few times of the day you'll get him all to yourself.)

**6:45** Make your bed and put a load of dirty clothes

into the washing machine. Open a book on the Great Masters and turn to a new painting by Rembrandt. Prop it in a recipe book holder on the hutch-dresser so the kids can look at it while they eat breakfast.

**7:00** Get the kids up for breakfast. If they are old enough to feed themselves take a cup of coffee into another room and sit there gathering strength for the onslaught of the day.

**7:30** Silly noises are escalating in the kitchen so that is the end of your break. You wipe the toddler's hands and face and tell the older children to get dressed. The baby is howling so you get him up and change his diaper.

**7:40** Put the baby in the jolly jumper, stop the toddler from eating the cat's biscuits, wash his face and hands again, and dress him. You won't like what you hear coming from the other end of the house.

"Hurry up and get dressed," you shout down the hallway, as you swing the grizzling toddler onto your hip. You tickle him under the chin. "Come and watch the birdies while Mummy hangs out the washing."

Mercifully, the grizzling turns off. You unload the washing machine with one arm and swing the washing basket onto your other hip before going out to the clothesline. You put the toddler down and hang out the washing.

**7:50** It is a great pity you don't have rear vision mirrors on the side of your head because awful things are happening behind your back. When you realize what's going on, you rush over and stop the toddler pulling out the seedlings you planted yesterday. Your mouth is a grim line as you stomp inside and wash his hands jerkily.

**8:00** The kids have had plenty of time to get dressed but when you check on them, they are half-naked. In exasperation, you finish dressing them. They are not the least bit grateful. They wail as sweatshirts go over their heads, and fuss as you hastily brush their hair.

**8:15** Start the kids on the dishes. Check the water is hot enough to wash the dishes without burning the kids. Although the plates won't be washed as well as you could wash them, they won't be too bad because the child drying the dishes will gleefully throw the dirty ones back in the water to annoy her sibling. Bang a time's-table-sing-a-long tape in the tape recorder (or the 2020 equivalent on your phone) so the kids hear it as they wash the dishes. Shovel the ingredients for bread into the bread maker and turn it on.

**8:30** Cut up vegetables and meat, load the crockpot and switch it onto slow.

**8:45** Tell the kids to, "hurry up and don't slop so much water around." Change the sheets in the toddler's cot.

**8:55** "Have you kids finished yet?"

"Yeeesss."

"Start making your beds then."

You inspect the kitchen and as usual, it is a mess.

"Come back, you haven't put away the dish wrack or wiped the bench." (You say it every morning and will continue saying it until they are twenty.)

They trail back. One slings the wet wrack into the cupboard while the other flicks a sodden cloth over a few spots on the bench. It is not good, but it's the best you are going to get without huge effort.

**9:00** "That will do, start making your beds," you say wearily, as the time's tables stop. You put the toddler on the potty.

"Do wees for Mummy," you say, as you pick the grizzling baby out of the jolly jumper.

This is likely to take a while so you feed the baby while you wait for the magical sound of tinkling, but after a quarter of an hour, the only sound is brim-brim noises as he runs a toy car over his bare leg.

**9:45** You put the baby under the baby gym.

"Alright, that will do," you say to the toddler, pulling his pants up and buttoning his overalls. You wash his hands and sit him on a tiny chair at a small table in the corner of the kitchen. "Make some pretty shapes." You pull a container of play dough out of the fridge and put it before him. "Mummy's going to see what your sisters are doing."

**9:50** You walk down the hallway and check on the bed making.

"How many times have I told you, you can't make a bed with something in your hand? Put the doll down and leave the cat alone. What is that big lump under the blanket?" You rip the bed open and find the sheets in a ball at the bottom of the bed. "No, don't just haul the blankets up, first smooth the sheets like this." You have shown them a thousand times before, but as faithfully as the sun comes up, the same old issues arise every morning.

**10:00** The beds are finally made. You stick gold stars on the chores chart after you open the curtains and put the baby down for his morning nap.

"Get out your dictation books," you say, as you whirl around the house straightening quilts and neatening rooms. Of course, they can't find them, but you are prepared for this regular emergency. "Here use this." You hand them each a sheet of paper and a pencil. You prop a simple reader open between the taps above the sink. "Jump Tip jump," you say slowly, as you wipe the bench properly. Your children (seated at the kitchen table) breathe heavily as, with tongues protruding, they grind their pencils laboriously over the paper. "Have you got that?"

"Yeesss."

"Run Tip run," you say, taking a broom out of the broom closet. While you sweep, small knuckles turn white as pencils start crawling across the paper again.

A horrible smell fills the room and you wish you had kept the toddler on the potty longer. Now he needs a complete change. You sweep the old crusts and dust bunnies into a dustpan and flick them into the bin. "Write your name while I change Johnny," you say, picking him up and heading for the bathroom.

**10:20** Johnny smells sweet again. You check the dictation and correct the mistakes.

**10:30** By now you are in desperate need of another cup of coffee. You give everyone a drink of milk and half an apple.

"Go and play outside," you say, as you scrape blobs of play dough back into its container and put it in the fridge.

**10:35** You carry your coffee through to the living room and slump on the couch. Outside, the toddler's ride-on-scooter rumbles back and forth along the veranda, and the springs of the trampoline squeak rhythmically as shrill voices laugh and sing. Peace, precious peace. You suck it up like expensive chocolate. By the time you drain your cup, the endorphins have risen. Everyone is safe, relatively clean, and happy. You are the queen of your castle and feel the satisfaction of running your household well. Unlike your children, the bread-maker gets on with its job without you having to hound it and a delicious smell is wafting through your neat and tidy house. You savour the ordered room you are sitting in because you know the shelf life of tidiness is fleeting.

**10:55** All too soon the lovely little bubble of peace pops as a fight breaks out. "Come inside and do some maths," you yell out the window. You put two pages of simple sums on the table and make sure they know how to do them before taking a little feather duster out of the broom closet.

"Do half the sums on the page and when you are finished, you can play a board game."

That should keep them occupied for an hour, which is how long it will take for the toddler to dust the small hall table. You pull up inner strength from the bottom of your soul as you prepare to engage in full-scale warfare. It is not that the job is too difficult for the two-year-old, wiping a tiny duster over a small table is hardly arduous. The issue is, who is the boss? It is you because he won't have the maturity to rule himself for many years, but he loudly and strenuously contests this idea.

"Dust the table, Johnny," you say, putting the duster in his hand.

He throws it on the floor and screams "NO."

"Alright, into the naughty corner you go."

You carry him kicking and screaming to a nearby corner and put him down facing the wall. He bawls and turns red in the face with rage. When he calms down, you take him back out of the corner, put him in front of the hall table, give him the duster again and repeat, "dust the table, Johnny." Once again, he drops the duster and shouts "NO." So it is back to the naughty corner. You yo-yo back and forth between the table and the corner for as long as it takes for you to win. The girls have long finished their sums and are deep into a game of Snakes and Ladders before Johnny finally yields to your authority and drags the duster across the top once. "Good boy, Johnny," you say hugging him. "That wasn't so bad, was it? You can go and play now."

Johnny toddles off happily to his blocks while you slump exhausted onto the couch. The baby has slept all through the hideous row because it is part of the routine. It happened yesterday, and the day before, and the week and month before that. You took the time to win today, just as you did all those other days, and tomorrow you will go through the whole process again until you prove beyond a shadow of a doubt, that you are the boss and a leader worth yielding to. As much as you would like to skip this daily battle, you keep going because you know once the battle is finally won, you will have laid the foundation for training, and saved yourself a truckload of trouble in the teenage years.

## Surviving Home-Schooling Through the Corona Crisis

I should get the girls to read to me, you think. But the mere thought of listening to shrill little voices stumble slowly through the antics of Janet and John and their jumping dog, Tip, sets your teeth on edge. You sigh. That is all the home-schooling that is going to happen today. Perhaps you can get some reading gone tomorrow if you do it first. Now is the time you might take the kids for a walk to the park to play on the swings and feed the ducks, but the lockdown has stopped all that. As you sit there a happy thought strikes you. You can sew a bit more of the quilt you are making. You glance at your watch. Eleven o'clock. Yes, there is time to squeeze in a bit before lunch. You lift your sewing machine onto the kitchen table.

"What are you making Mum?" asks your eldest daughter, pausing before she shakes the dice.
"A new quilt for your bed."
"Can I have one?" says Daughter Two.
"Yes, I will be making one for you as well."
"Can I make a quilt," says Daughter One.
"When you are older."
"Aw, I want to nowww."
The tone of her voice is sliding into a whine.
"Is that a whine I hear?" you ask, giving her the gimlet eye.
"No." She says it hastily, nervous that she has killed her chances of ever making a quilt.
"That's good," you say, softening your eyes and smiling.

The girls go back to their game as you on the other end of the table start piecing bright squares of fabric together. It is amazing how your energy rises as you do something you enjoy. Apart from an interruption caused by the baby, nothing disturbs your pleasure and morning swings along.

**11:30** You turn on the radio because it's time for your favourite program, Focus on the Family. The topic today is marriage. Although the game at the other end of the table is not finished, the girls abandon it as soon as the signature music sounds. On the back of their math's worksheets, they draw silently, their big ears flapping. Focus on the Family know all about flappy ears and kindly warn parents if something in the content is not appropriate for kids. Today there is no warning, so we all listen to five ways to strengthen our marriages.

**12:00** You turn off the radio, shake the bread out of its tin and make sandwiches. Because the table is occupied, you spread a tablecloth on the floor. "We are having a picnic today," you say giving them a plate of food. "Can someone give thanks for the food, please?"

Number One Daughter nods closes her eyes and rattles off, "thank you for this food dear Lord, amen."

They start munching while you take the baby out from under the baby gym. He is your fourth child so you are very skilful at doing things with one hand. You sit in a rocking chair nearby and feed him as you eat your lunch and drink your tea.

"Can I go outside and play?" asks Daughter Number two.

"For a little while."

They scamper off. You put the baby in the jolly jumper and he leaps and twirls in the doorframe as you wash the plates, shake the tablecloth outside, and whisk up any scattered crumbs.

When everything is tidy, you pick up the current reading book, Little House in the Bush, and pop your head out the window.

"Storytime."

The kid's feet make a thundering sound as they run inside. You take the baby out of the jumper and you all snuggle together on the couch as you read a chapter aloud.

**1:00** As you close the book, the moment you have been waiting for all morning is finally here. You put the baby and the toddler down for their afternoon sleep and open a large blanket chest.

"Chose one special toy and an activity for the afternoon," you say.

Daughter Number One chooses a colouring-in-book, crayons, and a bag of small dolls with tiny furniture.

(The doll's house is already in her room.) Daughter Number Two chooses blocks and dress-up clothes. Then you send them to their rooms with a stack of picture books.

"If you come out before I say you can, you will be cleaning the toilet," you say giving them the 'I-mean-what-I-say,' look.

They nod as you turn the audio book Hank the Cow Dog on for them to listen to as they play.

Oh, bliss! The next two hours are yours. The sound of bumblebees fills the house as you sip coffee and scroll through your phone. Now that the mothers of the nation are adjusting to the shock of the kids at home, complaints are being replaced with amazing activities. One woman posts a picture of her CLEAN kids (an accomplishment in itself) with their laver volcano. Another boasts that her four-year-old is reading fluently. A popular blogger writes; 'home-schooling is going fabulously. Last week the children did four-hundred worksheets. We learned all about geckos, and recycling, and built a scale model of the Eiffel Tower out of ten-thousand drinking straws.'

You compare these glowing reports with your pitiful efforts and feel the panic rising. How on earth am I going to get these children educated? you wonder.

**2:00** You are spiralling down into depression, so you put your phone away. You still have one precious hour and as it is an oestrogen day, you don't need to have an afternoon sleep. As soon as you start doing something you love, your mood lightens. By the end of the day, you will have something accomplished. It won't be as much as the woman who has hours of uninterrupted time, but at least it is something.

**3:00** What a pity the golden patch of the day is over.

"Tidy your rooms and pack all the afternoon things back in their box," you call down the hallway. "When you are done, you can have a drink and a biscuit."

The girls scrabble blocks and clothes, dolls and crayons, into a pile and dump them into the blanket chest before zooming into the kitchen.

"I hope you put everything back tidily," you say. Because you know it is a vain hope, you add, "I'm going to inspect."

The girls trail behind you with dragging feet. They stand with their hands behind their backs, staring at the floor as you whip the lid open and gaze at the jumbled mess stuffed in there. Although it is the same every day, you nevertheless feel your temper rising. If it had been a progesterone day, you would have blown your top and yelled a little. But because it is an oestrone day, you manage to stuff the internal yells down.

"Put all the clothes and dolls back in their bags," you say in grim tones. "If you dillydally and take too long, you won't be getting a cookie because it will be too close to dinner time."

**3:15** The kids have taken your threat seriously and the box is tidy. Why can't they do it properly the first time? You fume, handing them a cookie and drink of milk each. "Go outside and take Johnny with you," You say, keen to get them out of your hair.

You make a cup of tea and drink it while you feed the baby. Once again, the scooter rumbles along the veranda and the trampoline springs squeak. But this time, instead of feeling like a queen in her castle, you feel as if a semi-truck has run over you. You finish your tea and just sit there, swirling patterns in the baby's downy hair idly. The smell of the casserole wafts through the house and you are very glad you put it on earlier.

**3:25** Suddenly there is a commotion outside and you hear someone rush into the kitchen and rummage about in the cupboard.

"What are you looking for?" you call out.

"A jam jar and lunch paper, we've found the humungous-est centipede of the whole world."

"Huge, not humungous-est, humongous-est is not a word. Don't forget to punch holes in the lid so he can breathe and shut the cupboard door when you are finished."

"OK."

The cupboard door bangs and you hear the staccato of running feet. The bush outside the window rattles and there are shrill shrieks of excitement.

"He's behind that rock."
"Do centipedes bite?"
"I dunno, use the stick and flick him into the jar."
"Got him."
"Ooo, he's huge."
(You shudder slightly when you hear this.)
"Hold the jar while I put the rubber band around the paper."
"Don't forget the air holes."
Two soft pops sound as a fork punches through the taut paper lid. Three minutes later you are surrounded by excited kids.
"We found the world's biggest centipede," they shout, thrusting the jar within an inch of your nose.
You push the jar away from your face and take a good look at it.
"It is a whopper."
"What do centipedes eat Mummy?"
It is a teachable moment.
"They are carnivorous which means they eat meat. An animal or insect that is carnivorous is called a carnivore."
"Like a merry-go-round?"
"No, carnivore, not carnival."
"Do they eat steak?"

"No worms. Go and find some."
They rush off and peace descends.

**3:35** Now they have gone you feel instantly better as you realize you have almost an hour you at your disposal. You might get another strip of patchwork pieced together if you hurry. You put the baby in his bouncer net, carry him through to the kitchen and put the bouncer close to your chair.

"Here you are Bubby," you say, stuffing a rattle in his chubby fist. "Play with this while Mummy sews."

It works a treat. You hum as you stitch together patch after patch. Every so often when junior starts to fuss you joggle the bouncer with your free foot as you continue sewing.

**4:30** Alas, the hands on the clock on the kitchen wall tell you it's time to stop. You pack away your sewing before catching up the washing basket and marching outside. The kids are still digging dirt. Despite finding a worm, there is nothing to add to the jar as the toddler was the only one brave enough to pick it up.

"He was supposed to give it to the centipede," says Child Number One in a peeved tone, "but he ate it himself."

Because you are a seasoned mother, you shrug the calamity off. They have eaten worse. A worm is much better than the big stripy slugs that raid the cat's plate by the back door.

"Oh dear, never mind. Put the bikes in the garage and all the buckets and spades back in the sandpit," you say, as you pull the clean laundry off the line and fold it into the basket.

The kids push their bikes into the garage and chuck the sand toys into a heap on the sand. "Come inside everyone, wash the dirt off your hands and, girls, sort out the washing."

They follow you inside, and you dump the washing basket in the middle of the lounge. "Put all the socks into matching pairs. Then sort the towels into different colours and separate everyone's clothes into piles."

"What if we don't know whose clothes they are?" (They ask the same question every day and every day you give the same answer.)

"Just do your best. It's not hard to tell the difference between Daddy and Bubby's clothes."

While they do that, you catch the toddler and run the water for his bath as you undress him. Then you pop him in one end of the tub with all the water toys. He plays with his ducky and pours water from cup to cup while you bath the baby. Something about the pit hour makes the baby ornery. He likes his bath, but he fusses and howls as you dry him and button him into a clean stretch-and-grow.

"Have you finished sorting out the washing?" you call, as you run down the hallway with him.

"Yeeesssss."

Daughter Number two is a favourite with her little brothers which is a great help in moments like these.

"Play with Bubby while I bath Johnny," you say, thrusting the squalling infant into her arms before running back to the bathroom.

"Look at my puppets Bubby," she says, showing him the faces that she has drawn on her fingers. As she wiggles them and sings, he quietens down and you are left in peace to scrub all the grime off the toddler.

Finally, you are finished but Johnny wants more time to play in the water. Because your eldest daughter is old enough to be trusted with water safety, you ask her to watch over him while you thicken the casserole and put the piles of laundry away.

**5:00** Hallelujah, as you stuff the last towel in the linen cupboard, you hear the sound of your husband's car pulling into the driveway. You thank your daughter for looking after Johnny and lift him out of the water. He is about to howl because he does not want to get out but you distract him by saying:

"Daddy's home."

At the magical words, his crumpled face smooths into a

smile and he babbles "Dad-dad, Dad-dad."

As the backdoor squeaks open and your husband strides in, the kids swarm around him like a pack of excited dogs.

He picks the baby out of Daughter Number Two's arms and lifts him so he looks directly into his face. The baby dangles from between his father's large hands and his face splits into a gummy grin.

"Bub-bub-bub, dad-dad-dad, oo's daddy's wee man," your knight in shining armour babbles, pulling an exaggerated smiley face at the baby.

"Look at the humongous centipede we found Daddy," says Eldest Daughter proudly, thrusting the jar in his face. "It's carnival-est and eats worms."

"He has a million legs," says Daughter Number Two, "and I bet he's poisonous."

Johnny pulls his thumb out of his mouth. "My peed," he says solemnly.

The children's father peers into the jar and lets out a whistle of wonder when he sees the dangerous monster.

"I think you are very brave to catch the biggest centipede in the world," he says, looking at the girls admiringly and ruffling the small boy's hair. At this, all the children grow an inch taller. "Carnivorous, are they? He might like a worm to eat."

"We found one but Johnny was a carnivorous beast and ate it," says Daughter Number One, practising the new word as she glares at her brother.

"I think we should take a photo of him and put him back out in the garden."

"But I want to keep him forever."

"You could, but if you do, he will die. Would you like to die of hunger in a glass jar?"

The small mouths droop. "No."

"How about you show Daddy where you found him and let him go," you suggest brightly, "and for a special treat, I'll do your job of setting the table."

That whips the corners of the mouths up again and they all rush out.

**6:30** The centipede has gone back to the wilderness of the garden, dinner is over, and the two youngest are tucked up in bed. "Whose turn is it to choose the movie tonight?" you ask.

"Mine," says Daughter Number One.

You give her a choice between two movies. Even though you have kept it simple, she still has a bit of trouble choosing. While she is wavering, you whisk around the lounge tidying up stray blocks and toys. At last, she picks one and you slide it into the DVD player. The girls sit snuggled together on the couch and watch the screen enthralled. Meanwhile, you and your husband chat as you do the dishes and clean up the kitchen. Without your 'helpers' the job goes blissfully smoothly and quickly. Once everything is shipshape, you sit by the fire and chat about the day's activities. He moans about his boss and you complain about the kids in equal portions until the credits roll in the lounge.

**7:15** "Come on, kids. Time to clean your teeth and before bed."

They meander off to the bathroom and you oversee the teeth cleaning.

"That won't work, rub the brush over your teeth," you admonish, spotting a child poking a toothbrush in and out of a wide-open mouth without touching anything. "You don't want Bertie Germ to rot your teeth."

Your husband drops to his knees as soon as the nightly ritual of drink, toilet, and teeth is over. The kids squeal with excitement as they ride the bucking bronco to their beds. He tucks them into bed, prays for them and kisses them goodnight. Then he puts on an audio book and your children fall asleep listening to the stories you most treasure.

While he does this, you pull out your column cash books. Another day where virtually nothing got done. At least you did a bit of handwriting and maths.

You write 'letter formation' and 'addition' in the appropriate spot. You suck the end of your pencil. That's right, they looked at a picture while they ate breakfast.

'Viewed the Apostle Joe by Rembrandt' you write in the art column.

You suddenly remember the skimpy couple of sentences you dictated and smile. 'Dictation' you write and add 'sequential counting' in the box maths box when you remember the Snakes and Ladders game.

The centipede is a Godsend. You write 'explored the outside environment and studied insects,' with a flourish because it is not often you get to write anything in the science box. It may not be as impressive as a baking-soda-and-vinegar-volcano, but it took heaps less out of you and the kids liked it better.

Ah, huh! A wonderful thought strikes you and you write 'carnivorous and carnivore in the vocabulary box.

Bike, riding, jumping, running, tree climbing, go in the physical education slot.

What else? You think of the socks and towels and have a brainwave.

'Sorting objects into sets,' you write. Now you have three things in the math's box.

The health box is empty until you fill it with washing hands and cleaning teeth.

You are on a happy roll until you hit the reading. The reading is making you feel guilty. The longest line reserved for 'Books Read Aloud is alright,' you can record Little House in the Bush and Hank the Cow Dog there. It is the small slot for Early Readers that is bothering you.

I didn't listen to the girls read today you think guiltily.

Fortunately, you are distracted by the memory of the time's table tape. Now there are four things in the maths column. Your husband has finished putting the kids to bed, so you date it and rule the whole segment off.

As you view your day recorded in educational jargon, you realize much more happened than you initially thought. Moreover, it was accomplished with only a fraction of the stress that accompanies worksheets with LEARNING OBJECTIVES AND OUTCOMES.

In addition, you trained your children in the art of housekeeping, a skill they will use all their lives. You shut the book and file it in the junk drawer for tomorrow night.

**7:30** AT LAST! The rest of the evening is yours. You have your husband all to yourself. Sometimes you chat about your goals and dream about the future, building castles in the air. Other nights you watch a movie.

**9:30** You are in bed early these days because you need all the sleep you can get just to cope. As you drift into the twilight zone between wakefulness and sleep, the awful failure of NO READING haunts you. The guilt rises into a red monster and you know you are failing your children. Will your children ever be able to read and write? You wonder.

At ten at night, the answer is always negative. But the truth is, a day like this, followed by many variations of similar days, evolving as your children grow, is a more than adequate education.

# Summary

Of course, your home-school won't really look like this because every home-school is unique. If you have five rowdy boys, they may spend most of their time outside kicking a ball. The point is home-schools look vastly different to schools, and most days you won't get much done. Don't beat yourself up for your lack of busywork, because school teachers don't have to work twenty-four-seven, clean the school, cook the meals, deal with toddlers and babies, and wallpaper the room while they teach. If you are an average mother who loves her children, they will not be harmed by the closure of schools. Moreover, the chances are they will flourish and your family will grow closer.

# Beyond Corona

As I write, 2020 is not old and already it has been a momentous year. A couple of months ago bush fires ripped through Australia. Summer was like the backdrop of an apocalypse movie. Smoke hung in the air, turning the sky brown and the sun into a bright red disk. I went to bed fully dressed with my emergency bag at the side of the bed. As the fire front moved within mere miles of our home, roads were closed and emergency vehicles screamed up and down the highway. We did what we could; we cleared vegetation away from the house, blocked the drainpipes and filled the gutters with water, aware it was pitifully inadequate.

It was a stressful time and yet strangely wonderful. There was a sense of living through an epoch of Australian history.

"This is what it must have felt like in Britain in the second world war," I say to my husband. "The comradery is amazing."

As New Zealanders, we still don't know many people in the area where we live. We have been here for six years, but that is nothing.

"You have to be here thirty years before you are considered a local," people tell me over and over again.

That is until the bush fires. The bush fires break barriers. We meet neighbours we have never spoken to as we huddle at corners watching the fire engines flood into our street and station themselves in strategic spots.

Because this is my first bush fire, I am jittery.

"Is it time to leave now?" I ask the seasoned Australians.

"No, not if you are able-bodied, you need to patrol for flying cinders," says the man who lives in the house on the corner with the barking dog.

"The fire is still a distance away and the wind is expected to turn in an hour," says the lady from the A-frame house.

"How will we know when to go?"

"They will send a car through the streets with a siren and loudspeaker," says the man who drives a vintage car. "Then we go to the RSL."

## Surviving Home-Schooling Through the Corona Crisis

The man from the corner house pats his dog. "They do a good roast beef dinner at the RSL," he says, "and it's all free."

Evacuation suddenly seems quite fun and I am sure if we end up there our neighbourhood will huddle together in the crowded RSL. Perhaps by then we will swap names.

We don't go to the RSL, however, and I don't get a roast beef dinner either, because the wind changes and blows the fire away. As I unpack my bag, I realize afresh, people are the only things impossible to replace.

Although we could have got caught in a bush fire and died, in reality, the risk was not as high as it appeared. Certainly, nowhere as bad as it appeared on the 6 o'clock news. And because of the bushfires, I know my neighbours better.

Now hard on the heels of the bushfire comes the corona crisis. In momentous times like these, we can wallow in fear or watch with amazement the unfolding of a historic event. Unfortunately, many people are getting hit very hard with corona and dying, even as some people lost their lives in the bush fires. But just as most Australians did not burn to death, most of us will not get sick. For mothers of school children, struggles with naughty kids and elementary maths are likely the worst trials they will face.

Like the bush fires, this plague will pass, and most of

us will be alive long after it fizzles out. Unless we lose a loved one or fight on the front lines, we will quickly forget the difficulties. Instead, we will remember a special time when the world slowed down and everyone stayed home with their family, and neighbours chatted over their fences. Regardless of how you feel, your children and the family dog will think it was the best time of their life.

And even you, if you make a few adjustments, might find it is not the nightmare you expected. Irritating and frustrating for sure, but not a nightmare. And in years to come, your family will gather around the campfire, and reminisce fondly about home-schooling through the coronavirus, when you all (even Dad) stayed home, ate together, played games, camped in the backyard, and talked.

# About the Author

New Zealander Wendy Hamilton successfully home-schooled her four children from kindergarten through to university. Although Wendy is not superwoman and often struggles with low energy, her easy method of home-schooling enabled her to follow her interests while she trained her children. During these years she and her husband, Ian, renovated three cottages, and Wendy and her girls ran a patchwork shop in her home. In 2007 the whole family shifted to the USA. for eighteen months and in 2014 they moved to Australia.

Now her children are grown, Wendy spends her time writing and illustrating books.

# Books By Wendy Hamilton

*Eating a Light Bulb does not make you Bright*
Light on Home-schooling
*I told you not to Climb the Cactus.*
Surviving the Badlands of Motherhood
*Darling the Window is on Fire*
Love and House Renovations in New Zealand
*Homemade Church*

*Shipwrecks and Bush Felling*

## Children's Books

*The Britwhistles win a Prize*

*The Britwhistles and the Elasticizer*

*The Unlucky Snails*

*The Unlucky Snails go to France*
*Little House in the Bush*
Growing Up in New Zealand
*Little House in the Cow Paddock*
Growing Up in New Zealand

# Eating a Light Bulb does not make you Bright

## Light on Home-Schooling

### By Wendy Hamilton

Do your children struggle at school?

• Are you concerned they are being damaged in the school system?

You are not alone. with rising bullying, negative socialization, and moral decay, many parents are turning to home education as an alternative.

• But will home education disadvantage my children later in life?

• Do I need to be a qualified teacher to teach my children?

• How good is good enough?

With humor and transparent honesty, Wendy Hamilton addresses these and other concerns, through stories, and insights she gained, during her twenty-year journey as a home-schooling Mum. If you are considering home-schooling, currently homeschooling, or merely curious to peek behind a closed door, this is a book for you.

# Eating a Light Bulb does not make you Bright

## Reviews

★★★★★ 5 out of 5

**Filled with humor and honesty**

Amazon Verified Purchase

This book gives you a glimpse into a family engaging in something simple, yet extraordinary ... educating their children at home. Expect to relax, laugh, and ponder as you savor the wit and stories of an experienced homeschool mom as she recalls the little things that were truly the great things of raising her children. Whether or not you homeschool, or regardless of how long you have homeschooled, this book is an excellent read. Prepare for humor and honesty, and grab a copy today!

--------------------

**Homeschool Parent "Must Read"**

I have never EVER seen someone who "tells it like it is" with such humor! I have been a homeschooling parent for almost 20 years and the things that Wendy says are so true! I am having a struggle with helping my youngest (7) learn how to read and this book was so TIMELY and encouraging! It just reinforced the truth...modeling character, providing a rich learning environment, filled with love is what will make the difference in the long run. Most of my children learned to read later than expected and I didn't use formal curriculum...my kid in college is an A student, my son graduated from High School with honors...my 3rd child graduated from High School/Home school a year early. This was using the "lazy" method. EVERYTHING that you Read in this book is dead on truth....including how one feels about hearing boring prattle...LOVED IT! Keep writing Wendy. You are a gift!

--------------------

 5 out of 5

### Hilarious Home Schooling

Amazon Verified Purchase

I homeschool my daughter and thought this sounded interesting. I haven't finished it yet but am laughing so hard. Wish I had read this when I first started. I would have felt so much better.

--------------------

 5 out of 5

### Homeschooling mamas will relate and laugh like never before!

I loved how truthful the author is in this book. She makes you feel like you are sitting on the porch with her listening to the story. It is vibrant and full of laughter and truth of homeschooling. Any mama will relate to this mama and her worries and adventures. I could relate to the late reader and saw much of my own kids in hers.

A must read for some encouragement and laughs!

# I Told You Not to Climb the Cactus

Surviving the Badlands of Motherhood

By Wendy Hamilton

You do not have to be perfect to raise great kids you are more than enough.

Find the hidden leader within yourself that your children will look up to.

You have the power within you to fill your home with peace and harmony.

Your warm nurture is the perfect environment for raising small children.

With humor and transparent honesty, Wendy Hamilton addresses these and other concerns, through stories, and insights she gained, during her twenty-year journey as a home-schooling Mum. If you are considering home-schooling, currently homeschooling, or merely curious to peek behind a closed door, this is a book for you.

# Books by R.M. Hamilton
## Wendy's Daughter

### Lilly Gets Left Out

### A Very Good Wife Is Hard to Find

### The Candle Tree

### Boris Bottle the Late Bloomer

### Susie Solves the Case

### Diana and Her Crocodiles

### Henry and the Hot-Air Balloon

Henry Bogwasher has a secret! He's building a hot-air balloon with his friends to compete in the annual charity race. But can he win against the local bully, Oswald Orrid, and his super-duper store brought pirate-ship balloon?

CPSIA information can be obtained
at www.ICGtesting.com
Printed in the USA
LVHW092236140521
687512LV00001B/22